GOD Speaks Now of

A Seal Revealed

Anthony A Eddy

Cover Images

Front Image

The Statue of Liberty

where freedom reigns and the captives are set free.

Speaks of light, a tablet, a crown of thorns, an image,
a beacon to a nation, a herald to the world:
the supremacy—

of the agapé love of God.

***Scribal Note*:**
Refer Statue's Tablet inscription:
Shalom (Hebrew)— Peace, tranquility, wholeness, completeness, health, wealth,
prosperity, favour. The ability to finish. To be safe.
Nothing missing. Nothing broken. Nothing damaged.
"The Perfected World of God." Rec'd 3.30am, 7 Apr 2018
Refer also: 'Mountaintop of Life', Book 7, 'GOD Speaks to His Edifice'

— Internal Images —

Eternal Statements
with The Fiery Red Horse

Pages 5 & 96

Revelation 6:3-4 ³ When He opened the second seal, I heard the second living creature saying, "Come and see." ⁴ **Another horse, fiery red, went out.** And it was granted to the one who sat on it to take peace from the earth, and that people should kill one another; and there was given to him a great sword. *(Scribal emphasis)*

Scribal Note:
Refer to the Appendix for further related scripture references in The Book of Revelation.

Scripture taken from NEW SPIRIT FILLED LIFE Bible, the New King James Version®. (NKJV). Copyright © 1982 by Thomas Nelson. Used by permission. All rights reserved.

GOD Speaks Now of

The loving of man is at the head of His creation,
Where the variance of man tests the will of
the Holy Spirit as He brings the gifts
of God to dwell in His temple
now prepared and ready
for a child of God.

A Seal Revealed

So the agency of man needs a final resolution—
Sees man and his freewill, As he welcomes
freedom sharing his spirit and his soul:
Where there the two opponents
struggle with their conflicts
for a destiny in eternity.

Anthony A Eddy
(Scribe)

"When you are a child of God you change everything you touch."

Copyright and Publishing

© 2020 by BookWhip Publishing.

All rights reserved. No part of this publication may be reproduced, stored in a retrieval system or transmitted in any way by any means, electronic, mechanical, photocopy, recording or otherwise without the prior permission of the author except as provided by USA copyright law.

Printed in the United States of America

Soft Cover ISBN: 978-1-950596-20-1
Hard Cover ISBN: 978-1-950596-21-8
Ebook ISBN: 978-1-950596-22-5

9. "GOD Speaks Now of a Seal Revealed"

A Part of 'The End-time Psalms of God' as named by God, *or 'The End-time Homilies of God' as named by man - in being 'Religious discourses which are intended primarily for spiritual education rather than doctrinal instructions'*.

Cover design, Manuscript Content and Layout, Conceptual Related Imagery and titling texts, ©® Copyright May 2014, Jan 2016, Aug 2017, Apr 2018, 2019 by The Advent Charitable Trust, CC45056, Hamilton, New Zealand. All rights reserved worldwide.

www.thewebsiteofthelord.org.nz

Prepared on a 27in iMac™© with the use of Nisus®© Writer Pro. All trademarks™ and intellectual rights remain the property of their respective owners.

To order additional copies of this book, contact:
Bookwhip
1-855-339-3589
https://www.bookwhip.com

Prologue - 'Our GOD Loves'

Dedication

*To The Glory of God
and The Salvation of His People.*

*For our God of love, of justice,
of redemption
is very interested in all we do
and in our achieving our return home.*

He alone is worthy of the devotion of Man.

*I again have very real cause for gratitude in offering
the preparation of this book, both His first and last,
also into His care.*

———

*I am both exceptionally surprised and grateful—
for I live to see the day when a prize of God, which John held in his hand,
is released to be now shared with man from within the mystery of God.*

*The Scribe,
12.22pm Sunday 8th January 2017*

———

"This book represents The Ageing of Significance and not The Modernity of Today."

3.15pm Tuesday 7th May 2019

Acknowledgements

Here, acknowledgment of effort and thankfulness of heart is very much due to everyone who has helped in assisting in the completion of these nine books. I had no idea, when the first one started to come forth, that there were to be eight! And now a much earlier one has been found!

Current positions on personal privacy and its legal protection in many jurisdictions, to both wide and varying degrees, precludes their naming and public thanking. They are certainly deserving of full honouring for their efforts, and I am sure there are records written in the heavens that will, in due course, be declared.

One, however, does stand out above all others and due of very special honour and gratitude from a very thankful heart. Here I am speaking of The Lord Jesus, the Christ, with the Holy Spirit as sent to be with man, and of The Father who sent His Son to Earth.

May the fruit of everyone's work be blessed by The Lord within the lives of those in receipt of this and the other End-time Psalms of God. These may probably be better known by man in his naming as 'The End-time Homilies of God' - in being 'Religious discourses which are intended primarily for spiritual education rather than doctrinal instruction'.

May all be blessed by God as they witness this new beginning with the completing of the coming forth of an extensive and detailed end-time vision dictated in English by The Lord in these— His nine books.

May God, our loving Father, Jesus Christ, His Son, together with the Holy Spirit as our counsellor— bless and favour His wider family in all they do and bring to pass in the growth and development of His kingdom here in New Zealand and around the world. Marana tha— O Lord, come!

The Banner of the Kingdom was first flown as a flag at
10:30 a.m. on Monday, 1st September 2008
in Hamilton, New Zealand.
The Banner of the Kingdom was first flown as His flag on His church
in the village of Burripalem near Tenali, Andhra Pradesh, in India
on Sunday, 31st July 2011
in unity with Reaching Forward Ministries
of Tenali, Andhra Pradesh, India.

Forgotten Manuscript Discovered

This book's manuscript was dictated by The Lord between late 1989 and completion in early 1990. The manuscript gave rise to much difficulty after showing it to the Church Elders for they censored it as both blasphemous and thereby demonic in a church which neither accepted the gift of tongues nor of end-time Revelation. So this manuscript was never published nor offered for publishing and the two manuscript copies were placed in safe keeping with an eye to the future.

The earliest dated one was deposited in the National Bank at Whakatane, New Zealand, on Friday April 20th 1990 at 10.46 am. The second one dated 6th August 1990 was deposited with solicitors in Whakatane for the safekeeping of a backup. The texts themselves are both the same. This 'archiving period' was when all electronic copies were being destroyed on the computer as life moved on.

The manuscripts were removed from safe custody some two years later when my wife and I moved, for business reasons, to Hamilton, New Zealand.

The manuscripts spent years pigeonholed in a roll-top desk and followed us as we moved twice within this city's limits. When we downsized, the desk was sold and the envelope placed somewhat carelessly on my cramped office book shelves where it has lain for the last three years.

The two manuscripts copies were unexpectedly found while searching for a personal out-dated will; and the legal looking envelope had its two folded documents removed for examination: so the text has come to light some 26 years since it was received from God.

This book was originally received in seven chapters, with their titles which have been preserved, and seemed to be designed to be read continuously rather than in selected fragments. Within chapters some subtitles have now been added to enable more detailed indexing of the content's relevancy on a particular subject matter.

Capitalisation and punctuation are usually, but not always, at the scribe's discretion. The two words 'free' and 'will' have also been combined into 'freewill' as a single joined word with easier searching and conceptual understanding. The terms "mind of man" and "freewill of man" are indicated by The Lord as being fully interchangeable throughout the text here— both in context and in meaning. So also, at The Lord's request, the occurrence of the word 'beasts' is changed, when in the context of there being four, to 'living creatures'. This also maintains conformity of usage in all nine books within this series.

The text has been reformatted from 'flowing' to a 'prose' style in conforming with the eight other books where each is a part of the End-time Psalms of God. These may probably be better known by man in his naming as 'The End-time Homilies of God' - in being 'Religious discourses which are intended primarily for spiritual education rather than doctrinal instruction'. These started in 2007 and were completed in 2016.

The Scribe,
Thursday, 10th November 2016

Scribal Note:
"But many [who are] first will be last, and the last first. ..."

Matthew 19:30, 20:16; Mark 10:31, Luke 13:30

The context of the relevance of these scriptures in having application to this book, which now becomes the ninth part of the End-time Psalms of God, or as 'The End-time Homilies of God', is in being the first to be dictated in 1990 and the last to be published in 2017. So it seems to be, that in this instance—

The first will be last *in Order,* and the last first *in Importance.*
(Italicised words added)

Addenda: *After the above text was completed for inclusion in this book, a really severe surprise was still to surface in respect to this book's origin and history— so this is also recounted as received and dated from The Lord.*
9.30am Monday, 9th January 2017

Scripture taken from NEW SPIRIT FILLED LIFE Bible, the New King James Version®. (NKJV). Copyright © 1982 by Thomas Nelson. Used by permission. All rights reserved.

"This is the End-time of Faith."
7.12am Saturday, 12th November 2016

For Faith with Grace become fulfilled in the coming presence of The Lord.

My Content Study Aid

_____
_____
_____
_____
_____
_____
_____
_____
_____
_____
_____
_____
_____
_____
_____
_____

My Little Book

"This is the little book of which John writes.

It is My Alpha and Omega,
    My First and My Last,
    The Beginning and The End.

For now the seal is broken.

For now My little book is timed for release unto a hungry world.

For now My little book brings the demarcations of the eternal destinies of man.

For now My little book brings to the attention of man the bitter from the sweet—
        as it is placed upon the tongue of man,
        as it is digested for the nourishment of man,
        as it is sought for tasting as the end-time fare of man."

Received 2.22 – 2.37am Friday 6th January 2017

My Content Study Aid

_____
_____
_____
_____
_____
_____
_____
_____
_____
_____
_____
_____
_____
_____
_____
_____
_____

About My Little Book

"My little book has been held in readiness,
        has been kept secure,
        has the bespoke passages of God of both significance and earnestness.

My little book now comes forth to see the light of day among The Multitudes,
              among the seekers and the thoughtful,
              among the waiting and the ready,
              among the broken-hearted and the cheerless,
              among the hopeless and the lost—
                      both in their spirits and their souls.

My little book has been waiting a long time in the calendar of man,
        has been ready for release in the calendar of God,
        has been awaiting the end-time networking of man.

My little book releases the nuts and bolts of God which fit the spanners and the holes
                within the framework as held by man—
                that man may fit and tighten both My
                truth and righteousness within
                the home where they belong.

My little book is the chaperone to the soul,
        is the motivator to the spirit,
        is the backstop to a slide upon a slippery slope.

My little book points the way to a golden future,
        is the starting pistol held aloft in readiness to start a race,
        is the holder of the key points well worth remembering,
        is the release of the scent of The Spirit on a very dusty playground,
        is the caller-to-attention for serious consideration of the content held aloft:
                and now lowered into the outreached hands of man.

My little book has appeared before man in the past—
                when it was sampled by My disciple John
                      when on his island in the sea,
                      when on his island before Me,
                      when on his island for the record,
                      when with his record which survives before the
                            face of man for this very day.

My little book carries a mighty message—
        opens the initial thoughts of stardom;
        opens the possibility of a future of success
                      where the past is long forsaken—
                      where the future is being granted access;

        opens the thought patterns of man to consider
                the significance of his freewill;
                the significance of selecting a destiny of choice;
                the significance of all the implications depending
                      on his acting on his own freewill.

My little book is easily identified,
        is easily acquired,
        is easily read,
        is easily confirmed,
        is easily assessed,
        is easily assimilated,
        is easily understood with the message for today.

My little book is My blessing of The Multitudes—
                so all may have the opportunity to progress their lives
                      into their eternity of choice:
                either in companionship within the family of God
                or stagnant within the gates of hell.

My little book highlights the power of evil intent running rampant,
                          upon acceptance,
                          within the souls of man.

For there,
    within My little book,
        is contrasted the sweetness—
                to be found within the light as brought and shed by God;
        with the bitterness —
                as strewn around in the darkness by the works of Lucifer,
                      of Satan,
                      of the prince of darkness:
        as evidenced within the bounds of his deceit—
        the proliferation of the lies issuing from the mouth of man.
For Lucifer has long been and is removed,
                deposed,
                and dispossessed—
                from the counselling rooms of God.

My little book is an introduction to the godless of what a God should be,
        is either an introduction to where foresight leads to a great reward with
                                        an inheritance,
    or where rejection ultimately leads to a head filled with regrets—
                which negates an option no longer subject to a choice.

My little book is as an island floating on the river of life,
        is as an island visiting and departing,
        is as an island with a call—

        to hope and substance which can be grasped while all comes to rest:
           prior to again moving forward with the guiding current active—
        the other eight parts of The End-time Psalms of God*.

My little book has a season of fruitfulness,
        has a season of newness,
        has a season of expectancy and hope,
            of eventuality and trust,
            of both Faith and action,
            of when Grace is available and fully understood.

My little book carries the power of assignment:
        the power of truth revealed,
        the power of truth believed,
        the power of truth enacted—
        the power enabled from the cross,
        the power for the salvation of man,
        the power to establish the reconciliation of man with
                              The Loving Living God.

My little book is not now here to be ignored,
        is now here to catch the attention span of man,
            to blend the spirit of man over the soul of man,
            to blend the mortality of man in preparation with the eternity
                of man in his majesty of supremacy within creation—
                so to be fitted out in The Temple of My Spirit with
                            a heart in tune."

Received 10.54 – 11.43am, 12.55 – 1.28pm Saturday 7th January 2017

Scribal Note: *Refer* Book 2 'God Speaks to Man on The Internet' Revelation 10
or as 'The End-time Homilies of God'.

My Content Study Aid

_____
_____
_____
_____
_____
_____
_____
_____

Contents— Order Received

(2, 3, 4 ...) Denotes following items with a similar or same name as earlier ones

Title - God Speaks	I
Cover Image	II
Internal Images Fiery Red Horse	II
God Speaks Now of a Seal Rev	III
Copyright and Publishing	iV
Dedication	V
Acknowlegements	VI
Forgotten Manuscript	VII
My Little Book	1X
About My Little Book	X
Contents— Order Index	XIII
Contents— Alphabetical Index	XIV
Contents— Category Index	XV
My Book of Love	XVII
Appeal of Jesus (2)	XVIII
Introduction	XXI

Chap. 1   The Story of The Lord
- 01. Story of Our God   01
- 02. Song of The Servant   06

Chap. 2   The Love of The Lord
- 03. Love of Our God   07
- 04. Song of The Saved   12

Chap. 3   The Book of Life
- 05. Table of The Lord   13
- 06. Book of Life (2)— Records   16
- 07. Prayer of The Saved   20

Chap. 4   The Redemption of Man
- 08. Serving in Heaven   21
- 09. Freewill of Man (2)— spirit, flesh, soul, temple   23
- 10. Prayer of The Servant   26

Chap 5. Lang'es of Heaven & of Hell
- 11. Languages of Heaven   27
- 12. Fire of The Lord (2)   28
- 13. Tongue(s) of The S(s)pirit   29
- 14. Tongues of Angels   31
- 15. Tongues of Demons   32
- 16. Tongue of Lucifer   33
- 17. Functioning of Tongues   34
- 18. Actions of The Spirit   36
- 19. Tongue of Praise   39
- 20. Tongue of Worship   40
- 21. Tongue of Prayer   41
- 22. Song of The Lord   42

Chap. 6   The Destinies of Man
- 23. Sword of Vengeance   43
- 24. Call of The Lord   45
- 25. Fate of The Damned   48
- 26. Chariot of The Lord   49
- 27. Four Living Creatures   51
- 28. Lord Will Come   53
- 29. Gate To Life   55
- 30. Ways of The Spirit   57
- 31. Soul of God   60
- 32. Prayers of The Faithful   61
- 33. Prayers of Just & Unjust   62
- 34. Prayers of The Justified   63
- 35. Prayers of The Indwelt   64
- 36. Destiny of Lucifer   68
- 37. Prayer of The Lord   72

Chap. 7   Ordaining of The Servants
- 38. Spirit Structures   73
- 39. Banner of The Cross   75
- 40. Record of The Spirit   77
- 41. Faith of The People   79
- 42. Triumvirate of God   81

Appendix—   88
- Tongues of Man   89
- Tongues of Demons (2)   91
- Revelation 6:1-8 plus Others   92
- *Horses, Riders, Creatures*   93
- End-time Summary of God   94
- *Journaling and Notes (1)*   96
- *Journaling and Notes (2)*   97
- *About the Scribe*   98
- Epilogue - 'Our GOD Lives'   99
- The End-time Psalms of God   100
- *or The End-time Homilies of God*
- 4 End-time Flowers of God   101
- Synopses 4 Flowers of God   101

Contents— Alphabetical

(2, 3, 4 ...) Denotes following items with a similar or same name as earlier ones

Title - God Speaks	I
Cover Image	II
Internal Images Fiery Red Horse	II
God Speaks Now of a Seal Rev	III
Copyright and Publishing	iV
Dedication	V
Acknowledgements	VI
Forgotten Manuscript	VII
My Little Book	1X
About My Little Book	X
Contents— Order Index	XIII
Contents— Alphabetical Index	XIV
Contents— Category Index	XV
My Book of Love	XVII
Appeal of Jesus (2)	XVIII
Introduction	XXI

A
18. Actions of The Spirit	36

B
39. Banner of The Cross	75
06. Book of Life (2)— Records	16

C
24. Call of The Lord	45
26. Chariot of The Lord	49

D
36. Destiny of Lucifer	68

F
41. Faith of The People	79
25. Fate of The Damned	48
12. Fire of The Lord (2)	28
27. Four Living Creatures	51
09. Freewill of Man (2)— spirit, flesh, soul, temple	23
17. Functioning of Tongues	34

G
29. Gate To Life	55

L
11. Languages of Heaven	27
28. Lord Will Come	53
03. Love of Our God	07

P
37. Prayer of The Lord	72
07. Prayer of The Saved	20
10. Prayer of The Servant	26
32. Prayers of The Faithful	61
33. Prayers of Just & Unjust	62
35. Prayers of The Indwelt	64
34. Prayers of The Justified	63

R
40. Record of The Spirit	77

S
08. Serving in Heaven	21
22. Song of The Lord	42
04. Song of The Saved	12
02. Song of The Servant	06
31. Soul of God	60
38. Spirit Structures	73
01. Story of Our God	01
23. Sword of Vengeance	43

T
05. Table of The Lord	13
16. Tongue of Lucifer	33
19. Tongue of Praise	39
21. Tongue of Prayer	41
20. Tongue of Worship	40
14. Tongues of Angels	31
15. Tongues of Demons	32
13. Tongue(s) of The S(s)pirit	29
42. Triumvirate of God	81

W
30. Ways of The Spirit	57

Appendix—	88
Tongues of Man	89
Tongues of Demons (2)	91
Revelation 6:1-8 plus Others	92
Horses, Riders, Creatures	93
End-time Summary of God	94
Journaling and Notes (1)	96
Journaling and Notes (2)	97
About the Scribe	98
Epilogue - 'Our GOD Lives'	99
The End-time Psalms of God	100
or The End-time Homilies of God	
4 End-time Flowers of God	101
Synopses 4 Flowers of God	101

Contents— Category

(2, 3, 4 ...) Denotes following items with a similar or same name as earlier ones

Title - God Speaks	I
Cover Image	II
Internal Images Fiery Red Horse	II
God Speaks Now of a Seal Rev	III
Copyright and Publishing	iV
Dedication	V
Acknowledgements	VI
Forgotten Manuscript	VII
My Little Book	IX
About My Little Book	X
Contents— Order Index	XIII
Contents— Alphabetical Index	XIV
Contents— Category Index	XV
My Book of Love	XVII
Appeal of Jesus (2)	XVIII
Introduction	XXI

My Creation (1)
36. Destiny of Lucifer	71

My Grace (2)
06. Book of Life (2)— Records	16
08. Serving in Heaven	21

My Love (7)
My Book of Lov	XVI
01. Story of Our God	01
03. Love of Our God	07
05. Table of The Lord	13
09. Freewill of Man (2)— spirit, flesh, soul, temple	23
22. Song of The Lord	45
30. Ways of The Spirit	60
37. Prayer of The Lord	75

My Return (3)
26. Chariot of The Lord	52
27. Four Living Creatures	54
28. Lord Will Come	56

Preparation (10)
11. Languages of Heaven	27
12. Fire of The Lord (2)	28
18. Actions of The Spirit	39
23. Sword of Vengeance	46
24. Call of The Lord	48
29. Gate To Life	58
31. Soul of God	63

35. Prayers of The Indwelt	67
38. Spirit Structures	76
40. Record of The Spirit	80

Thanksgiving of Man (7)
02. Song of The Servant	06
04. Song of The Saved	12
07. Prayer of The Saved	20
10. Prayer of The Servant	26
32. Prayers of The Faithful	64
33. Prayers of Just & Unjust	65
34. Prayers of The Justified	66

The Cross (1)
39. Banner of The Cross	78

The End-time (2)
Appeal of Jesus (2)	XVII
25. Fate of The Damned	51
41. Faith of The People	82

The Trinity (1)
42. Triumvirate of God	84

Tongues (8)
13. Tongue(s) of The S(s)pirit	29
14. Tongues of Angels	31
15. Tongues of Demons	32
16. Tongue of Lucifer	33
17. Functioning of Tongues	34
19. Tongue of Praise	42
20. Tongue of Worship	43
21. Tongue of Prayer	44

Appendix—	88
Tongues of Man	89
Tongues of Demons (2)	91
Revelation 6:1-8 plus Others	92
Horses, Riders, Creatures	93
End-time Summary of God	94
Journaling and Notes (1) & (2)	96 & 97
About the Scribe	98
Epilogue - 'Our GOD Lives'	99
The End-time Psalms of God	100
or The End-time Homilies of God	
4 End-time Flowers of God	101
Synopses 4 Flowers of God	101

My Book of Love *(Dated early 1990)*

"This book,
    My book of love,
        has been written,
    as received,
    by My servant,
        Anthony.
    He has recorded faithfully and without error The Words I spoke to him in order that My intent may be made known to man.

    My intent is that none should perish through not knowing of The Will of The Father.

    It is for this purpose and to confirm the end-time that I now speak through
            My prophets;
        that all may be warned of the plans of Lucifer;
        that all may know of the love of The Lord;
        that all may know of the work of The Father.

O,
    People of The Lord,
        arise,
        serve.
        Read and understand.
        Read and believe.
        Read and act.

For the gate is swinging shut on those who do not know the Saviour of the world;
    the gate is swinging shut to the glee of Lucifer;
    the gate is swinging shut at the end of the Time of Grace.

I,
    The Lord God of Israel,
    The Risen King,
    the Doer of The Father's Will,
    the Redeemer of mankind would have this known this day."

My Content Study Aid

_____
_____
_____
_____
_____

The Appeal of Jesus (2)

"These end-time books,
  these parts of the end-time Psalms of God*,
    I,
      The Lord Jesus,
        have dictated to My willing servant,
                Anthony.

These end-time Psalms of God* highlight the behaviour of man,
                highlight the streaming ways of Heaven,
                highlight the testing of man,
                highlight the call for man,
                highlight the eternities of man,
                highlight the preparation of man,
                highlight the protocols of Heaven,
                highlight the love of God for man,
                highlight the adoption of man into the family of God.

These end-time Psalms of God* accompany My word of ages,
                My scriptures recorded for the advantaging of man,
                My inter-relationship with man in his development
                          upon The Earth.

These end-time Psalms of God* are intended to have availability to The Multitudes,
                are intended to indicate the greater things to come,
                are presented so that man may not deny the presence of
                    his God in the surroundings as gifted to man—
                    whereon he is formed in the image of
                          The Living Loving God.

  I,
    The Lord Jesus,
      love and certify My people,
      love and intermingle with My people,
      love and greet My people—
        in every conversation open for participation by man seen in his glory
                in reaching for the stars.

  I,
    The Lord Jesus,
      love and confirm My people,
      love and support My people,
      love and dwell within My people—
        as they convert their flesh lives into The Temples of the spirit,
              into The Temples of My Spirit,
              into The Temples of God—

        with each containing their personal Ark of the New Covenant:
            where each holds a committed heart of God—
              to be carried right back home—
                into the familiarity of their spirit's birthing in
                    the dwelling place of God.

I,
   The Lord Jesus,
      love and magnify My people,
      love and cherish My people,
      love and welcome My people to their home within the stars—
              to their home prepared,
              to their home of wonder and delight,
              to their home of peace and serenity.

I,
   The Lord Jesus,
      treasure and esteem the capabilities of My people,
      circle and appreciate the crafts of My people,
      examine and uphold The Glory of My People—
          as they arise in body soul and spirit to the claiming of their inheritance,
                to the claiming of their jewels as
                    stored and waiting,
                to the prospects established for their
                  new life within eternity—
                in the companionship of God.

I,
   The Lord Jesus,
      would welcome each one home—
              from the time within The Multitudes,
              from the time within mortality,
              from the time bespoke for preparation,
              from the time of learning in the university of God,
              from the time of assimilation into The Kingdom of God,
              from the time of Faith with Grace,
              from the time where My people stared at the stars—
                  and wondered what they held.

I,
   The Lord Jesus,
     encourage and tug at the heart of man—
  to commit to an everlasting journey through the doorways of Faith and Grace.

    For by such are the scopes and venues of eternity reached.

    For by such are the gates of Heaven opened in anticipation.

    For by such is the beckoning of God.

    For by such may the pathway to God be trod by man.

For by such will the promises of God be fulfilled within the eternity of man."

Gratefully received from The Lord for use in this— both His first and ninth book.

*These may probably be better known by man in his naming as 'The End-time Homilies of God' - in being 'Religious discourses which are intended primarily for spiritual education rather than doctrinal instruction'.

The Scribe, 6.30 – 7.32 am Monday 19th December 2016

My Content Study Aid

_____
_____
_____
_____
_____
_____
_____
_____
_____
_____
_____
_____
_____
_____
_____
_____
_____
_____
_____
_____
_____
_____
_____
_____
_____
_____
_____

Introduction

This divine text mostly consist of truth statements intermixed with counselling and is presented for serious contemplation as to the ramifications and how we approach the text in the conclusions we may draw. For it is filled with great significance for these present times.

I testify here to one and all that these books are neither of my writing nor instigation but rather have arisen from the dictated word of God. This book is comprised of seven chapters. The original document is a continuous text received from God. Please take it, therefore, as a 'given' as to the stated origin both by testimony and by claim.

The style of the book preserves any scribal notes in italics; while double quotation marks ("...") indicates subdivided text of a divine origin. In this series "'cross'" within the text is not usually capitalized as the means of The Lord's death, being treated as similar to a knife or a sword. However in this particular book it is used as a part of a significant title e.g. "'Banner of The Cross'"; and is capitalized. British spelling is used for reasons of national culture. Each subdivided part may be accurately searched from within His website. A concordance or a thesaurus has not been used at any stage prior to, during, or after the receiving of these texts. A dictionary (Oxford Concise™) has sometimes been used to comprehend fully, The Words of the divine voice used in expressing His intent. Because of the means of receipt, the punctuation is subject to human interpretation. Minor spelling "'typos'" are scribal, and the titles usually are also. Multiple subjects sometimes occur in a particular chapter, which may preclude a single title being entirely appropriate in terms of descriptive accuracy.

Attached to the end of most items is 'My Content Study Aid' inserted at the request of The Lord Jesus to enhance the benefits found in meditating on and understanding the 'Hows' and 'Whys' of the truth statements and His counselling as found herein. If no such Study Aid exists at the end of an item then there are additional Journaling & Notes pages provided in the Appendix. Please remember this is your book to use in the way which best serves your growth within the discipleship of God.

Great care was taken to ensure the initial scribal accuracy in that earlier hearing and transcribing. And now also in the rescanning and revalidating of the typed original document in the optical scanning process— which has resulted in these printed pages of divinely originated text. Every word is as received without later omissions, additions, substitutions, or edits— except as already mentioned in regards to 'freewill of man' and the 'living creatures' on the earlier 'manuscript' pages which also record The Lord's assent in each instance.

May the Holy Spirit so testify as such to every enquiring soul. All rights reserved.

"This is the End-time of Faith."

7.12am Saturday, 12th November 2016

For Faith with Grace become fulfilled in the coming presence of The Lord.

Chapter 1: The Story of The Lord

The Story of Our God

"In the beginning was The Word,
    and The Word was throughout the firmament,
    and the firmament grew both in size and in stature,
            until The Word decreed—
                that all things that had been created were to The Glory of God.

Then the Kingdom of the universe became a blessing to all mankind.

The Glory of The Word came to dwell with men,
    and the heavens were opened,
    and men began to commune with angels,
    and great was the rejoicing both on Earth and in Heaven—
            for The Glory of The Word had become known to man.

The Word opened His heart,
    and The Glory known to man fell on all the face of The Earth,
    and all creatures knew The Word and rejoiced.

Then the heavens were opened,
    and The Word decreed—
              that from that time forth all of creation would know and
                        worship God.

Then The Word spoke throughout all the heavens,
    and glory came upon the faces of the angels as they prayed,
    and worshipped The Word,
    and The Word blessed them for they had seen the face of The Word,
    and The Word dwelt amongst them from that time forth.

Then The Word opened His mouth,
    and spoke to the nations of The Earth giving them words of praise—
              that they might glorify their creator,
    and the nations of The Earth offered their praises to the heavens,
    and The Glory of The Word came and dwelt amongst them.

Then The Word proffered His hand to the peoples of The Earth,
    and peace fell upon the nations.

The Word opened His heart to the peoples of the nations,
    and The Glory of The Lord was made known to all nations.

The Lord spoke to the peoples in their own languages,
    and gave them instructions in the way they should live,
    and many nations listened to The Word of The Lord,
    and they blessed Him as their nations grew and prospered.

Then The Lord opened His mouth again,
    and decreed that all nations on the face of The Earth,
        all creatures,
    and all the forces of nature should bow before Him as He moved across the face of
                                                            The Earth.

The Lord spoke to the peoples,
    and called some by name that they might give the message of The Lord—
                      to all those who would listen,
    and The Spirit of The Lord moved in the hearts of those people—
        that they might bring forth The Word of The Lord:
        to all those who would listen to The Law of The Lord.

Then the peoples of the nations rebelled against those people called by The Lord—
                      and did not honour them.

The Lord spoke again,
    and decreed that those nations that did not honour the people called by The Lord
        would come to naught;
        the nations that from their beginning had praised and worshipped
            The Lord had rejected The Lord's Anointed
        as they ministered to their people.

Now The Lord spoke again,
    and the heavens were opened and The Lord ministered to the people,
        as He moved across the face of The Earth in power and majesty:
            nations heard Him and bowed before Him;
            nations trembled;
            nations humbled themselves;
            nations wept and cried to The Lord:
    and The Glory of The Lord abounded in those who heard The Words of The Lord.

Then The Lord spoke to the angels of Heaven,
    and instructed them in all things pertaining to the hearts of men—
        that the angels might minister according to the needs of men,
    and they were sent forth to all corners of The Earth to minister the love of God to
        the peoples of The Earth.
    And the peoples of The Earth rejoiced when The Word of The Lord was revealed
        to them,
    and the angels returned to the gates of Heaven praising God as they brought the
        news of the doings of men.

All creation groaned as The Spirit of The Lord was grieved.

The Lord raised His arm and moved upon the face of The Earth,
    and His angels were summoned before The Throne of Grace,
    and were instructed according to The Will of The Lord.

The Throne of Grace resolved the things of The Father.

The Father called His angels by name,
    and they approached the Most High in obedience to His Will.

The Father moved in power,
    and the angels bowed before Him as they were instructed in the battle plan
                                                    against Lucifer.

The Father raised His arm,
    and decreed that from that day all those upon The Earth would receive knowledge
                            of The Lord,
                            The Son of The Father,
                            The Anointed One,
                            The Risen King,
              The Saviour of the world through signs and wonders assigned to
                            those who carried The Word of The Lord.

Now The Lord expressed The Will of The Father throughout the heavens,
    and,
        as the heavens rejoiced,
        Lucifer resolved to fight the armies of The Lord;
        those called by The Lord to testify on Earth—
        that Jesus The Christ had risen from the dead—
        and now reigns with The Father.

The Spirit of The Lord,
The Glory of The Lord,
        accompanied the armies of The Lord as they battled the demons and the fallen
                                  angels sent against them by Lucifer.

The armies of The Lord went forth accompanied by the angelic hosts assigned to them by
                                                            The Throne of Grace.

The angelic hosts moved with haste as they served the armies of The Lord;
    and they moved over all The Earth doing The Will of The Lord.

The armies of The Lord preached The Word to the nations of The Earth
                                    as The Lord directed them,
                                    as The Lord led them,
                                  and as The Lord instructed the angels.

Then The Lord surveyed His armies,
                testing them for their Faith and their obedience,
                      and for their willingness and ability to listen.

Many were found wanting;
        for they did not listen;
        for they did not obey;
    and they were unaware of The Will of The Lord.

Those who fell,
 those who had been snared by the agents of Lucifer,
                    were ministered to by The Spirit of The Lord.

Some rejoined the battle,
            clothed again in the full armour of God,
                                The Eternal Father.

Some left the battle and bemoaned their fate as they watched the battle rage around them.

Some joined the powers of darkness,
        the agents of Lucifer,
    and then fought against the very anointed of The Lord;
    and their stupidity was recorded.

And they who gathered around the thrones conferred with those in authority concerning
                    the progress of the battle.

And they were sent forth on chariots of fire to carry the battle to Lucifer anew;
                to tend the fallen of The Lord;
                to mend the broken hearts;
                to revive the down-trodden spirits;
                to uplift the banner-carriers;
                to sound the trumpet-calls;
            and to be with those who were committed to the fight.

The Spirit of The Lord fell afresh upon the warriors of The Lord:
                those who had heard the trumpet-calls;
                those who were in the battle;
                those who were laying-waste the works of Lucifer;
                and they fought with courage—
                    as they used the weapons they had been given.

The warriors of The Lord carried the battle for the control of The Freewill of men to all
                    the corners of The Earth.

    They fought against the forces of Lucifer:
                the men who feed the demons;
                the men who have turned from God;
                the men who worship Lucifer.
    And women also were found who sought rewards from Lucifer,
                and they were numbered with the men.

Those with Lucifer were many.

They were united in their greed.

Their resources were vast.

Their authority and influence extended all over The Earth.

And they abused The Earth:
> My footstool;
> My creation;
> as they raped and pillaged and plundered the things of God.

And the peoples of The Earth,
> save a few,
> consented."

My Content Study Aid

The Song of The Servant

"I praise Your name,
        O Lord.

For mighty are Your works on The Earth.

Mighty are Your works before the angels.

Mighty are Your works over Lucifer.

Mighty are Your works before Man."

My Content Study Aid

_____
_____
_____
_____
_____
_____
_____
_____
_____
_____
_____
_____
_____
_____
_____
_____
_____
_____
_____
_____
_____
_____
_____
_____

Chapter 2: The Love of The Lord

The Love of Our God

"Then I,
    The Lord,
        gave a new weapon to My warriors—
            a weapon that would turn the tide of battle—
            a weapon to vanquish the forces arrayed against My people—
            a weapon to use against those whose Freewill is imprisoned—
            a weapon that will set the captives free—
            a weapon that will demolish the strongholds of Lucifer.
        In the hearts of My people I then embedded My weapon—
                                    the weapon of Love.

For I,
    The Lord,
        want My people to know that love conquers all;
                love is all there is to life;
                love is what holds the world together;
                love is in the spirit of man;
                love is the conqueror of man's soul;
                love is the delight of The Lord;
                love fears nothing;
                love overcomes all:
                love knows the truth;
                love sees into every soul;
                love is the happiness in the lives of men;
                love is the essence of The Lord;
                love is displayed in all creation;
                love surrounds the thrones;
                love is The Son in The Father;
                love redeems the world;
                love saves mankind;
                love lasts throughout eternity;
          and when the angels bow before the thrones love guides
                        and directs them every time.

For The Spirit,
    The Comforter,
        will,
        in love,
        keep My people.

And in love My people will speak My Words.

And,
> with love,
> My people will teach the peoples of The Earth to know Me—
>> > The Risen King,
>> > and My love.

And,
> in love,
> My people will impart the messages The Spirit will plant within their hearts.

And it is for the love of the peoples of The Earth that The Spirit would direct My people
> > > every day.

And The Love of The Lord shall be with My people.

O,
> The Love of The Lord shall be with My people.

And they will bring The Message of Love to mankind.

For I,
> the First-Born,
>> will have A Church of Love on The Earth;
>>> that men may know the love that is within My heart.

And love will magnify and grow,
> and the people will have love for one another,
> and they will love each other as never before.

For The Spirit will put love within their hearts like they have never known before.

And they will come with rejoicing in their hearts;
> as they praise and worship and love The Risen King.

For I love My people.
> O,
>> I love them so.

And now the love of The Father shall be made known to His people.

And the love of The Risen King shall instruct The Spirit of The Lord concerning the
> > > hearts of men.

> And some will walk in love,
> and some will walk in Faith,
> and they will all rejoice.

My Word on Earth;
My Word in Heaven;
My Word throughout eternity shall be directed by My Spirit.

I have spoken to the prophets,
I am speaking to the prophets,
and I shall speak to the prophets.

And when they walk with Me,
    and when they talk with Me,
    and when they bring forth My messages to men,
        they shall honour Me:
                The Lord,
                The Risen Saviour,
                The King of mankind,
                The Alpha and the Omega,
                The Everlasting Lamb,
                The Saviour of the world,
                The Son of The Eternal Father.
        And I shall exalt Him;
        and He loves Me;
        and I shall do His Will.

And before the thrones of man will go The Prophets of The Lord.

    And they will testify of Me.
        They will do My work.

    And thrones of man will fall.
        Empires will split.

And those who do not love The Lord will fear His wrath.

    For I control the elements;
        and through them I will teach those who do not fear The Lord of their iniquity.

    For when they sin they will reap the harvest of their sins,
        but I would show them mercy whenever they turn from them;
            for I love them all the days.

    But they shall not come against The Saints of God.

        They shall not battle them.

        They shall not fight them.

I will protect My Saints on Earth from the works of Lucifer.

    They go forth,
    in My name,
    to the nations of The Earth;
    and they carry My Banner of love with them.

    They carry My Banner on high and with it they will crush the plans of Lucifer.

    They will walk in boldness.

And they will preach the message of love as they go before the thrones of nations.

Those who hear shall be gathered close to Me and those who reject Me shall be given to Lucifer.

O,
    I would have them all come to Me.

    But I know the hearts of men.

    I know their will.

    I gave them their freedom for them to walk their way.

    I would have them be with Me through all eternity,
            and it grieves My heart when I see their sin and what they do to what I created:
            what they do to My creation;
            what they do to one another.

                It breaks My heart.

  For I love them and I would that they be redeemed from their sin.

But,
    My people,
        understand;
        I am The Son of Love.

        Love is just and fair.

        Love is kind and forgiving.

        Love is always there.

So,
    in justice and in love,
            I will punish sin.

    In sorrow and in mercy,
            I will forgive it.

    In joy and in thanksgiving,
            I shall reward those who follow Me.

For The Message of Love shall be proclaimed;
    The Message of Love shall go forth to the nations;
           that the sifting may be complete.

For I will sift the nations,
        the peoples of the nations,
        the cities of the peoples,
        the households of the cities,
        the families of the households.

    I will sift each family.

For as the miller sifts the flour so shall I sift the people of The Earth.

> As the miller selects the wheat to blend the flour,
> as the baker selects the flour to form the dough,
> and as the dough is left to become the risen loaf—
> so shall The Spirit prepare the people of The Lord."

My Content Study Aid

The Song of The Saved

Now,
    The Lord has shown to me,
                  this day,
Of how The Father cared for Him
With love that has defied The Cross.

For there He shredded all my sins
That I may now rejoice
In The Love of The Risen King.

As I commune with Him,
With The Spirit on my tongue,
I know that He instructs me in His ways.

For my praises soar,
Borne by The Spirit of The Lord,
To the highest courts of The King of Kings.

And there my words are recorded;
And they shall testify
Of my love for The Lord.

And they shall there exalt
His works and His deeds—
Those given me to do while here on Earth.

And now I worship you,
    O God,
That you may surely know—
My heart,
    with love,
I have surrendered:
To The Glory of The Lord—
    my Risen King!

And all Creation praised and prayed:
"Amen and Amen!"

My Content Study Aid

_____
_____
_____

Chapter 3: The Book of Life

The Table of The Lord

"The Bread Of Life has now been broken before the face of man;
                               the face of man now has seen the
                                         suffering in the world.

The Bread Of Life has now been subject to The Will of He who sent Him;
                               The Will of He who sent Him is now known.

The Bread Of Life now is calling from The Throne on high;
                               The Throne on high that now commands the
                                         attention of mankind.
    For if all of man would taste the bread that is spread before them now,
                               the bread I have prepared for eating at The Banquet of
                                             The Lord,
                           then they would surely come to the table now prepared.

                                 But all of man will not taste of;
                                 all of man will not come to;
                                 all of man will not be at—
                                                 The Table of The Lord.

The Table of The Lord is now prepared for those who love The Lord.

    Seated at the table will be those who have served The Father;
    seated at the table will be those who have served The Son;
    and seated at the table will be those invited by The Spirit.

There,
    they will partake of The Covering of The Lord—
            all that has been declared to which they are the heirs—
        that they may receive the fullness of their inheritance.

    The inheritance composed of The Blessings of The Lord;
                      The Promises of The Lord;
                      and The Reservations of The Lord.

    For then shall The Lord keep His Word to His people:
                    The Word received by Faith,
                          acted on in trust,
                          stored up in the heart,
                          and shared with love.

    Then those gathered before The Lord,
                    at the table of The Lord,

            will rejoice in their inheritance.

They will be thrilled with their inheritance.

They will be overjoyed at what they have received at the table of The Lord.

For there they will receive,
           according to the record,
                      the reward for suffering;
                      the reward for persecution;
                      the reward for faithfulness;
                      the reward for service;
                      the reward for sacrifice.

There,
   they will receive the reward of the presence of The Lord.

At the table of The Lord the hungry will be fed by The Spirit as they kneel in the presence of The Lord.

Those who are not hungry will leave the table of The Lord unaccompanied by The Spirit.

Those not invited will attempt to overturn the Table of The Lord as they do the will of Lucifer.

Then the hungry will have their reward for seeking the things of The Kingdom of God;
           for their hunger will remain;
                their eyes will be opened;
                their hearts will be filled with the Love of The Lord;
                their hands will then serve;
                their feet will then walk;
                    and their tongues will then bear testimony of The Son.

Then I,
    The Lord,
        will uplift those who would serve,
            those who would go,
            and those who would tell.

For I would have willing servants—
                joyful,
                loving,
                kind—
                        empowered by The Spirit and committed,
                        walking in The Spirit and rejoicing,
                        accompanied by The Spirit and proclaiming.

My message to the nations,
My word to the nations,
My glad-tidings to the nations will be taken by My willing servants now.

The message will be carried by My willing,
> eager,
> loving,
> caring,
> hungry servants now:
>> the hungry servants fed at The Table of The Lord;
>> The Servants that hunger for My Word;
>> The Servants that hunger for the Light;
>> The Servants that hunger to serve.

And The Table of The Lord will travel with the servants of The Lord.
> The Table of The Lord,
> The Banquet of The Lord,
> The Supper of The Lord—
>> will be set before the people;
>>> the people due an inheritance from The Lord.
> The people,
>> there made welcome to The Kingdom of The Lord,
>> rejoicing,
>> singing,
>> dancing,
>> will then regard their former ways;
>>> their sinful paths;
>>>> their wayward walks as now no longer in The Record of the Lamb.

For there,
> at The Supper of The Lord,
>> The Spirit will confirm The Lamb's acceptance of their sins,
>> The Spirit will confirm the sacrifice of love,
>> The Spirit will confirm the removal of the references to their sins from The Record of the Lamb."

My Content Study Aid

_____
_____
_____
_____
_____
_____
_____

The Book of Life— The Records of God

"The Book of Life,
   The Record of The Lamb,
   The Tome of all Creation,
               contains the works of God.

   Therein written are all things past,
             all things that are and all things yet to be.

   All creative acts are there recorded;
            each created intelligence is there recorded;
            each act of created intelligence is there recorded,
                    that the record be complete.

This,
   The Record of The Father,
   The Record of The Son,
   The Record of The Spirit,
            is now revealed,
              in part,
              to man.

The Book of Life contains the love of God,
         declares the love of God,
         records the love of God.

   The love of God is all of His creation.

   The love of God is displayed—
              for all to see that see,
              for all to hear that hear,
              for all to touch that touch,
              for all to smell that smell,
              for all that sense to sense—
                 that all that know,
                    may know.

The Record of The Father,
        therein written,
        details the plan for man.

The Record of The Son,
        therein written,
        details the birth of man.

The Record of The Spirit details the ascent of man,
        is yet to be recorded,

                in its fullness in The Book of Life.

The Record of The Father,
        now revealed,
        is the history of creation.

The Record of The Son,
        now revealed,
        declares God's love for man.

The Record of The Spirit,
        now revealed in part,
        decides the fate of man.

The Book of Life was sealed but now the seal is broken by The Spirit.

The Spirit breaks the seal in the presence of The Father and The Son.

The Spirit now reveals man's walk,
        in Faith,
        to God.

The Spirit now reveals God's walk,
        in Love,
        with man.

The Spirit now reveals man's destiny with God.

The Spirit now reveals the end of times.

    For The Spirit now would uphold The Word of The Father and The Son.

The Record of The Father and The Son contain The Glory of The Spirit made manifest
                                                                                          to man.

The Record of The Spirit confirms the life of man.

    The records all contain the love of God for man,
                            God's encouragement of man,
                            the sacrifice of God not stopped by man.

The Records of the Angels record the love of man for man.

    The record of each angel holds the deeds and words and thoughts of each man,
                        as assigned,
                        as he deals with his fellow man each day.

The Records of the Angels may not be changed.
    Once written,
        their records stand.

    Once written,
        their testimony is established.

Once written,
> their evidence is available before the courts on high.

The Record of The Spirit details the motives of man,
> the reasonings of man,
> the excuses of man,
>> in the presence of his God.

For,
> from times past,
> The Spirit has declared the reality of God before created man.

The Spirit has declared the authority of The Lord—
> the Living Christ,
> The Word as sanctified to all mankind.

The Record of The Spirit may be opened before The Thrones on High.

The Record of The Spirit details the extent to which man has resisted Lucifer,
> details the extent to which man has embraced Lucifer,
> details the extent to which man has followed God.

The Record of The Spirit may be called by man,
> may be used by man,
> may justify man.

The Record of The Spirit is not written,
> may be changed,
> follows the life of man.

The Record of The Spirit declares the worth of man before the courts when called and
> before the thrones when asked.

The Record of The Son states the sacrifice of God,
> states the teaching of man,
> states the intent of The Son.

The intent of The Son has been made known:
> it is that none should perish—
>> that all should come before the thrones;
> it is that all should know The Father—
>> and His love;
> it is that all should be empowered by The Spirit—
>> as a testimony of The Risen King.

For the intent of The Son is to redeem all of man:
> to draw all to Himself and to then present them to The Father—
>> all those entrusted to His care.

The Record of The Son has now been written in the heart of man,
> now exists in the library of the heavens.

The Record of The Son will exalt The Father,
> declares The Will of God through all eternity,
> states the victory over Lucifer.

The Record of The Son intercedes for those in need,
> intercedes for those made captive,
> intercedes for those condemned.

The Record of The Son portrays the whole of time,
> continues the Record of The Father,
> fulfills The promise of The Father,
> destroys the angel of death,
> describes The Coming of The Spirit,
> supports The Prophets,
> upholds The Father.

The Record of The Son testifies with The Spirit at the judgement of man.

> And there,
>> at the judgement of man,
>>> will all the books be opened;
>>> all the records inspected;
>>> all the testimonies made known—
>>>> for nothing shall be hidden from The Throne of Grace—
>>>>> that each man may be judged according to what has been established before the courts on high."

My Content Study Aid

_____
_____
_____
_____
_____
_____
_____
_____
_____
_____
_____
_____
_____
_____

The Prayer of The Saved

"O Jesus,
>The Living Christ,
>Come,
>now,
>in Your Glory.

Reconcile all of Your Blood-bought creation.

Let The Spirit dwell with us this day that we may walk with Him.

Help us to understand Your Word to man.

Give us,
>this day,
>The Faith to thwart the plans of Lucifer.

Lead us through the fires of torment and affliction.

Bless us with Your Grace,
>and endow us with Your Authority:
>As You meet our needs this day."

My Content Study Aid

Chapter 4: The Redemption of Man

Serving in Heaven

"The Throne of Grace will plead for man before The Throne of White.

The Throne of White will judge according to the law that decrees justice.

The Throne of White decides the fate of man after The Spirit speaks.

    The speaking of The Spirit will not condone the sins of man.

    The Record of The Son shall pardon those who love The Lord.

    Those who love The Lord may call on The Spirit to reveal the love they there profess.

    And there the justice of The Throne of White will be tempered by the mercy of The Throne of Grace.

The Throne of Grace receives the evidence of the Angels,
    the evidence of man,
        and the evidence of The Spirit concerning the works of man on Earth—
            those done in the name of The Risen King;
            those done under the hand of The Father;
            those done by the guidance of The Spirit.

The Throne of Grace acknowledges the works of man arising from the love of man for God.

The Throne of Grace conducts the affairs of Heaven,
    as written in The Record of The Father,
    in conjunction with The Father and The Spirit.

The Throne of Grace is the seat of authority of The Risen King,
    The Alpha and the Omega,
    The Messiah of the Jews,
    The Light of the Gentiles,
    The Sacrificial Lamb,
    The First-born of The Father,
    The Teacher of Man,
    The Image of The Father,
    The Shepherd of the Flock,
    The Intercessor for the Flock,
    The Blood-bought Son of The Living God that now reigns.

Around The Throne is gathered those who serve in Heaven—
    all those under the authority of The Son.

Those who serve in Heaven are the spirits of the dead—
> those who died in service to The King—
> those awaiting the resurrection of their bodies—
> those who are the heirs of The Father—
> those who loved The Lord while on Earth.
> And there,
> while serving,
> > they learn the laws of Heaven that they themselves may
> > > rule in righteousness.

Those who serve in Heaven have stood before The Throne of White—
> have been before the courts,
> have been confirmed by their angels,
> > upheld by The Son,
> > > endorsed by The Spirit and approved by The Father.

Those who serve in Heaven are the children of God,
> are the redeemed of The Lord,
> > are awaiting the resurrection of their bodies when the graves
> > > are opened at the shouting of The Lord.

For when the graves are opened by the shouting of The Lord The Love of God shall
> raise all those asleep.

The love of God shall lift the dead and,
> united with their spirits,
> reclaim them from the fall of man.

The fall of man has invoked the penalties for sin.

The soul of man will not survive the death of the Flesh—
> may not come into the courts of praise,
> dies with the flesh.

The corruption of the flesh relates to the soul of man;
> corruption of the soul of man ensures its death.

Death is ensured by The Will of God.

Death of the flesh is the inheritance of man arising from the fall of man.

> Man fell when man first disobeyed the instructions of The Lord;
> man will ascend when each acknowledges The Call of The Lord.

The Call of The Lord reaches into the soul of man.
The soul of man reacts to the Call of The Lord.

The soul of man is established at his birth—
> his birth on The Earth created by The Son—
> his birth on The Earth by woman—
> his birth on The Earth which fulfills the plan of God."

The Freewill of Man— spirit, flesh, soul, temple

"The freewill of man is established during his life in the flesh,
    proceeds beyond the grave of the flesh,
    is nourished by the flesh.

  The freewill of man reasons;
    seeks;
    explores;
    discerns;
    learns;
    acquires.

  The freewill of man retains;
    recalls;
    judges;
    knows;
    creates;
    dwells.

The *freewill* of man continues.

The freewill of *man* continues.

The freewill of man *continues*.

The freewill of man is judged.

The freewill of man is united with the spirit of man when the flesh is born.

The spirit of man is the conscience of man that dwells within the flesh.

The spirit of man was established by decree of The Lord;
    was present with The Lord prior to the birth of man;
    guides The Freewill of man.

The spirit of man is nourished from The Spirit on High,
    is subject to The Freewill of man,
    opposes the soul of man,
    survives the passing of the flesh,
    carries The Freewill of man to the very presence of The Lord.

The spirit of man conflicts with the soul of man;
    The Freewill of man has dominion over both.

  The Freewill of man can choose.

  The choice affects the destiny of man.

  The act of choice confirms the freedom of man.

The freedom of man is confirmed by the deeds of man;
>> is confirmed through The Words of man;
>> is confirmed of God.

The death of the flesh is in the plan of God.

The death of the flesh destroys the soul of man.

The soul of man aligns with Lucifer—
> is the seat of deceit within the flesh;
> tortures the spirit of man;
> denies the existence of God;
> forswears accountability.

The soul of man would lead The Freewill of man—
> would prevent The Knowledge of The Spirit.

The soul of man pronounces the lie that leads to the second death;
>> the second death—
>> the death of the spirit of man—
>> is the objective of the soul of man,
>> that The Freewill of man may not attain its place of
>>> Righteousness before The Lord.

The spirit of man commands the angels from on high to record the intent of the soul
>>> of man,
>>> the will of The Freewill of
>>> man and the actions
>>> of the flesh of man.

The freewill of man proceeds beyond the grave of the spirit.

The freewill of man may redeem the spirit from the grave;
> needs to redeem the spirit from the grave;
> should redeem the spirit from the grave.

The freewill of man in knowing God redeems the spirit from the grave—
>> the spirit that has borne him thus so far.

The spirit,
> the spirit of man,
>> that confirms the Call of The Lord to The Freewill of man;
>> that guides The Freewill of man;
>> that carries The Freewill of man:
>>> then needs The Saving Freewill of man.

The freewill of man,
> The Saviour of his spirit,
> will then be clothed in Righteousness before The Lord.

The Temple of The Flesh will then become The Temple of The Spirit.

The Temple of The Spirit will not know decay;
> has a new name;
> enacts The Will of resurrected man;
> contains The Freewill of man;
> must contain the spirit of man.

The spirit of man will then read The Book of Life to The Freewill of man.

The Book of Life shall then disclose the plan of God for man;
> shall then disclose the eternities to man."

My Content Study Aid

The Prayer of The Servant

"O Jesus,
    The Risen Christ,
    The Saviour,
    The Redeemer:
May my soul be under the control of my Freewill;
May my spirit be set free to soar to The Thrones of Heaven;
May my Freewill commend all things of The Spirit.

May my flesh be empowered to serve The Risen King;
May the angels minister according to The Will of Heaven;
May The Spirit come,
        bringing The Fire of Heaven to The Earth.

May The Throne of Grace call in mercy;
May The Throne of White judge in justice;
May this—
    Your servant—
        know,
        and do:
            The Will of God this day."

My Content Study Aid

_____
_____
_____
_____
_____
_____
_____
_____
_____
_____
_____
_____
_____
_____
_____
_____

Chapter 5: Languages of Heaven and of Hell

The Languages of Heaven

"The Languages of The Spirit delight in The Lord,
        delight with the angels,
        delight with the spirit of man.

The tongues of The Spirit are designed for man,
        to uplift his spirit,
        to encourage him,
        to commune with God.

The tongues of The Spirit are bequeathed by The Spirit to The Freewill of man.

As each would ask so each shall receive;
        enquire so each shall be answered;
        learn so each shall be taught;
        acquire so each becomes filled.

The Spirit of The Lord indwells those who love The Lord.

The Spirit,
The Holy Spirit,
The Holy Ghost,
    baptizes with fire only those who so desire;
        only those who so seek;
        only those who so pray;
        only those who so ask:
        only those who so confess—
            The Fire of The Lord in their hearts."

My Content Study Aid

_____
_____
_____
_____
_____
_____
_____
_____

The Fire of The Lord

"The Fire of The Lord indwells The Freewill of man;
    indwells the spirit of man;
        does not impact on the soul of man.

The Fire of The Lord does not speak for man until man surrenders control of the flesh.

For when man yields control The Fire will spread throughout the flesh:
        giving Glory to The Son,
        giving Honour to The Son,
        giving Praises to The Son,
          and Talking to The Son.

The Fire of The Lord uplifts the spirit of man,
    brings the soul into submission,
    emboldens The Freewill of man,
    does not suffer injustice from the soul of man.

The Fire of The Lord,
The Zeal of The Lord,
    burns in the heart of man.

The Fire of The Lord consumes the hatred of the heart;
    consumes the envy of the heart;
    consumes the malice of the heart;
    consumes the anger of the heart;
    consumes the dross of the heart—
        the dross of the heart—
            so-called by man."

My Content Study Aid

The Tongue(s) of The S(s)pirit

"The tongues of man are spoken by The Freewill of man.

  The tongues of The Spirit are spoken by the spirit of man.

The tongues of man are spoken by man to man.

The tongues of The Spirit are spoken by The Spirit to the spirit.

The tongues of man inform man.

The tongues of The Spirit inform the spirit.

The tongues of the spirit of man converse with The Spirit on High.
                        converse via The Spirit with man;
                        converse in the spirit with man;
                        converse in The Spirit with God.

The tongues of the spirit of man may converse with the animals;
                        may converse with the birds;
                        may converse with the elements;
                        may converse with demons;
                        may converse with Lucifer;
                        may converse with angels;
                        may converse according to The Will of The Lord.

The tongues of the spirit of man may converse with man in the tongues of man.

The tongues of the spirit of man may converse when The Fire of The Lord burns within
                                            The Freewill of man,
                                            the heart of man,
                                            the being of man,
                                            in a Temple of the flesh
                                                      that is surrendered.

The tongues of The Spirit are given by The Spirit under the direction of The Lord.
                    They are given by The Spirit to fulfill The Promise of The Son;
                              to prepare The Freewill of man;
                              to disclose the power of God.

The freewill of man accepts The Spirit's tongue—
                    when The Freewill of man is subject to The Will of The Lord;
                    when the soul of man is subject to the spirit of man;
                    when the ears of man are opened to The Word of The Lord.

The freewill of man knows The Spirit's tongue—
                    when The Spirit so reveals;
                    when called by God to impart His word to man;

when the white stallion and the rider dressed in white call
all those who love The Lord;
after the death of the flesh;
as the language of Heaven;
through his experience with God.

The tongue of The Spirit relates the praise of the spirit;
relates the worth of The Freewill;
relates the state of the soul.

The tongue of The Spirit relates the health of man.

The tongue of The Spirit conveys the thoughts of man.

The tongue of The Spirit ordains The Word of The Lord,
speaks The Word of The Lord,
acknowledges The Word of The Lord,
upholds The Word of The Lord.

The tongue of The Spirit is the ecstasy of The Lord;
the servant of The Lord;
the voice of The Lord.

The tongue of The Spirit brings the message of The Lord.

The tongue of The Spirit confesses the sins of man;
verifies the state of man;
reproaches the soul of man;
continues with man;
laughs with man;
cries with man.

The tongue of The Spirit testifies to man,
of man,
and for man.

The tongue of the spirit—
the spirit of man—
commands the attention of the angels and the courts on high;
develops with man;
matures with man;
lives with man.

The tongue of the spirit will remain with man."

My Content Study Aid

_____

_____

The Tongues of Angels

"When The Lord speaks the angels praise in tongues given them by God.

The tongues of angels sing to the thrones on high,
           chatter as they bring the news from Earth,
           whisper as they see the works of God.

The tongues of angels murmur as they witness the works of Beelzebub:
                       The Prince of Darkness;
                       The Antichrist;
                       The Destroyer;
                       The Archangel that Fell.

Witnessing the works of Lucifer causes the tongues of the angels to murmur before God.

When the angelic tongues are heard a hush falls over Heaven—
               as the angels bow,
                      reporting;
               as the angels depart,
                      rejoicing;
               so the record of man is established by the
                      angels every day.

When the angelic tongues are heard a peal of bells ring out—
               welcoming the spirit;
               welcoming The Freewill;
               welcoming the spirit and Freewill of man.

When the angelic tongues are heard a trumpet blasts.

   The trumpet blasts when man is judged and accepted by The Throne of White;
                       accepted by The Throne of Grace;
                       accepted by The Thrones on High.

   The trumpet blasts when man is welcomed into the realms of Heaven.

The angelic tongues are heard reporting man."

My Content Study Aid

_____

_____

_____

_____

The Tongues of Demons

"The tongues of demons decry The Lord,
        exalt man,
        will not praise The Risen King,
        are silenced by God,
        renounce the spirit of man,
        deny the onward passage of man,
        condemn the soul of man.

The tongues of demons lie,
        shout,
        doubt,
        mimic the tongue of Lucifer.

The tongues of demons reveal the soul of man;
          the iniquity of man;
    gloat.

The tongues of demons reveal the lusts of man;
          the malice of man;
    recount.

The tongues of demons reveal their intent;
          their attributes;
    sin."

My Content Study Aid

_____
_____
_____
_____
_____
_____
_____
_____
_____
_____
_____
_____

The Tongue of Lucifer

"The tongue of Lucifer commands the demons—
        demands obedience from the demons,
        does not uphold the demons,
        cannot be trusted by any of creation,
        is worn with bitterness,
        mouths its frustration,
        writhes in hate.

The tongue of Lucifer rejoices at the Lost;
        rejoices at the lie believed;
        rejoices at the deception planned;
        rejoices at the lie confirmed;
        rejoices at creating doubt;
        rejoices at the destruction of The Saints.

The tongue of Lucifer will be silenced,
        may be banished,
        need not be heard,
        exalts Lucifer.

The tongue of Lucifer hinders the work of God.

The tongue of Lucifer may not prevent the work of God.

The tongue of Lucifer revels in greed;
        in pride;
        in envy;
        in sexual immorality;
        in bestiality;
        in linkage not of God.

The tongue of Lucifer will not stand.

The tongue of Lucifer is already condemned.

The tongue of Lucifer shall be brought to account."

My Content Study Aid

_____
_____
_____
_____

The Functioning of Tongues

"The tongues of The Spirit are for the benefit of man.

The tongues of the spirit,
        the spirit of man,
                are for praise;
                for worship;
                and for prayer.

The tongues of The Spirit are for confession;
                      for conversing;
                      for enquiry.

The tongues of The Spirit are The Glory of Heaven.

The tongues of the spirit of man number three.

The tongues of The Spirit may not be numbered by man.

The tongues of the spirits are known to God.

Tongues of man cannot speak the tongues of Heaven without the agreement of The Spirit.

Tongues of man,
    numbered in thousands,
    are learnt by man.

Tongues of The Spirit,
    unnumbered by man,
    are taught by God.

Tongues of the spirit of man,
    numbered by Three,
    are heard by God.

All tongues of The Spirit are spoken in love;
                      are spoken with love;
                      are spoken through love.

Love,
    the adhesive of the tongues of The Spirit,
    commands the attention of the soul of man.

The soul of man speaks with tongues of demons,
        acquires the tongues of demons from Lucifer,
        speaks the tongues of demons incessantly.

Man may not understand the tongues of demons,
    suffers the tongues of demons,
    may embrace the tongues of demons.

The tongues of demons are not heard in the courts of praise.

The tongues of demons capture The Freewill;
        antagonize the spirit of man;
        repel the approach of The Spirit.

The Spirit approaches,
   demons repel;
   God waits.

The tongues of demons are silenced by the Fire of The Spirit,
        the Fire of The Lord,
        the Zeal of The Lord.

The Fire of The Spirit comes to men through Faith to receive,
        through the decree of The Lord,
        through the ministry of man.

The Fire of The Spirit carries the tongues of The Spirit to the spirit of man.

The Fire of The Spirit may be seen by man,
        may be heard by man,
        may be smelt by man."

My Content Study Aid

_____
_____
_____
_____
_____
_____
_____
_____
_____
_____
_____
_____
_____
_____
_____
_____
_____

The Actions of The Spirit

"The Spirit,
    The Holy Spirit,
    The Baptizer of the spirit of man,
        confirms the work of The Spirit by anointing The Freewill;
            by anointing the flesh;
            by anointing the spirit.

The Spirit anoints those who would stand before The Lord in supplication.

The Spirit leads those who would be led;
    guides those who would be guided;
    speaks through those who have surrendered.

The Spirit would lead the surrendered flesh.

The Spirit anoints the broken-hearted,
    anoints the contrite,
    anoints the confessed,
    anoints all those who bow the knee before The Lord.

The Spirit knows The Freewill of man,
    knows the spirit of man,
    knows the flesh of man.

The Spirit does not know the soul of man.

The Spirit teaches man of woman in the empowering of the spirit,
    testifies to man of woman by the empowering of the spirit,
    works through man of woman with the empowering of the spirit.

The empowering of the spirit,
      the spirit of man,
        will move man of woman to testify of God.

The Spirit comes on the wind of Heaven,
      bringing God to man,
      at the behest of The Father.

The Spirit,
The Holy Ghost,
The Comforter,
    comes as arrayed before the thrones,
      so arrayed before the angels,
      to array The Freewill of man.

The Spirit comes to allay the fears of man.

The Spirit moves with The Fire of The Lord,
                The Fire of The Spirit,
                The Empowering of God.

The Spirit moves over the face of the chosen of The Lord,
                over the peoples of the nations,
                over the face of The Earth.

The Spirit moves among the dung hills of the cities,
                among the mansions on the hills,
                among The Multitudes of man.

For when The Spirit moves The Freewill of man will wonder,
                The Freewill of man will judge,
                The Freewill of man may come to know The Lord.

When The Spirit moves man's destiny is changed;
                man's destiny is changed by the moving of The Spirit;
                the moving of The Spirit changes the destiny of man.

The Spirit moves in power,
                in wrath and by decree.

The Spirit moves in love,
                in gentleness and by prayer.

The Spirit moves in authority,
                in subservience and by ministry.

The Spirit hears the pleadings of the people,
            hears the cries of the lost,
            hears the blasphemies from The Freewill of man.

The Spirit is grieved when forced to listen to the voice of man.

The Spirit listens to instructions from on high,
            listens for the tongues of Saints in prayer,
           listens at the prayer-room of the heart.

The listening of The Spirit consoles the heart of man.

The Spirit does The Will of The Father and The Son,
            does progress the plan for man,
            does decide the destiny of man.

When deciding,
            The Spirit examines The Freewill and spirit of man.

The Spirit acts to thwart the plans of Lucifer,
            acts in the interests of man,
           acts in fellowship with The Father and The Son,
           acts in love,

acts with compassion,
acts through authority.

The Spirit,
 The Baptizer of the Beloved,
 The Marshal of the Hosts,
            calls The Fire of Heaven down on Earth."

My Content Study Aid

The Tongue of Praise

"The Tongue of Praise is intelligible to the angels.

The tongue of praise frequents the thrones,
        silences the angels,
            uplifts those who serve in Heaven.

The tongue of praise is heard,
        is welcomed,
        is written.

The tongue of praise emanates from The Freewill of man.

The tongue of praise speaks of man's appreciation of creation,
                      of the revelations of The Lord,
                      of what God has done for man.

The tongue of praise sings;
        rejoices;
        lauds—
        the tongue of praise fears the work of God.

The tongue of praise approves;
        commends;
        thanks—
        the tongue of praise loves the work of God.

The tongue of praise accepts;
        enjoys;
        endorses—
        the tongue of praise approves the work of God.

The tongue of praise is spoken by the spirit from The Freewill to The Thrones on High."

My Content Study Aid

_____
_____
_____
_____
_____
_____
_____

The Tongue of Worship

"The Tongue of Worship is heard only by The Thrones.

The tongue of worship is directed to The Thrones,
        is received by The Thrones,
        is acknowledged at The Thrones.

At the thrones the tongue of worship is recorded in The Book of Life.

The tongue of worship loves;
        weeps;
        is in awe—
        the tongue of worship is spoken to the presence of The Lord.

The tongue of worship senses;
        knows;
        honours—
        the tongue of worship is spoken to the presence of The Spirit.

The tongue of worship prostrates;
        magnifies;
        elevates—
        the tongue of worship is brought before the presence of
                              The Father.

God,
    The Father:
God,
    The Son:
God,
    the Holy Spirit—
        all respond in unison when the tongue of worship speaks."

My Content Study Aid

_____
_____
_____
_____
_____
_____
_____

The Tongue of Prayer

"The Tongue of Prayer is carried by the angels,
                is repeated by the angels.

The tongue of prayer is a sacred trust.

The tongue of prayer seeks;
                yearns:
                pleads—
                the tongue of prayer wants action from The Thrones.

The tongue of prayer requests;
                repeats;
                upholds—
                the tongue of prayer supports the action of The Thrones.

The tongue of prayer intercedes;
                accepts;
                believes—
                the tongue of prayer expects action from The Thrones.

The tongue of prayer spoken by the spirit,
                subject to The Freewill,
                carried by the angels,
                is answered according to The Will of God.

The tongue of prayer is answered,
                is tested,
                is heard.

The tongue of prayer,
                when answered,
                affects the destiny of man;
                affects the destiny of all created things;
                affects the relationship of man and God."

My Content Study Aid

_____
_____
_____
_____
_____

The Song of The Lord

"I,
  The Lord,
    will take the land from those who would destroy it.

I,
  The Lord,
    will rest upon the land that is bequeathed.

I,
  The Lord,
    will protect the land from those who would so conquer.

I,
  The Lord,
    will uphold those who dwell in the city of the great God.

Come now,
    with rejoicing,
        as you enter the gates with praise.

Come now,
    with dancing and with singing,
        into the temple courts.

Come now,
    with thanksgiving,
        as The Lord Your God so calls.

For the people of The Lord shall be blessed.

For the people of The Lord shall be free.

For the people of The Lord shall be called.

For the people of The Lord shall be saved.

Enter with joy into the walled city of The Great God.

Enter with love into the streets once seared by the tears of The Living Lord.

Enter with sorrow into the citadels of the city that now blaspheme.

Witness to each nation of this consecrated land.

Witness to each land of this dedicated city.

Witness to each city of this Glory of The Lamb.

Witness to each lamb of this offering of The Lord."

Chapter 6: The Destinies of Man

The Sword of Vengeance

"The Lord came upon the people in power,
>>and defended them with The Word,
>>and transfixed them with the sword,
>>and commended them with prayer.

The people,
> seeing the power of God,
> fell to the ground in awe and worshipped Him.

The people on the ground were spared,
>>were blessed,
>>>were counted as the children of God.

The people who dared to stand before the power of God had the sword withdrawn and
>>>>they no longer heard from their God.

Then another sword was sent by The Lord,
>>carried by an angel,
>>held aloft and on fire,
>>with a 'V' emblazoned on its blade.

And it was wielded with the authority of the One who sent the angel,
> it had two edges,
> it had not been used before,
> it shone and gleamed,
> it was not sheathed,
> it was ready to be used.

The Lord surveyed His people,
>>those still standing on their feet,
>>and His heart was grieved at what He was about to do.

> For they would not repent;
>> they would not listen to the servants;
>> they would not receive the sovereignty of God.

The angel heard the commanded word of God and the sword,
>>>once held aloft,
>>>moved in a sweeping curve.

> Few there were who stood before their God.

The angel sheathed the sword that now was wet.

The sword that no longer burned with fire was sheathed.

Sheathed was the sword now carried by the angel.

The angel of The Lord returned the sword to Heaven.

The angels who saw the sword wept and cried in shame that their charges had not
responded to their Lord.

The Father took the sword now proffered by the angel and returned it to the armoury
of God.

The sword now sheathed is resting in the armoury of God,
    in waiting is resting in the armoury of God,
    in readiness remains within the armoury of God.

The sword of vengeance rests.

The sword of vengeance waits.

The sword of vengeance will be used again. And again. And again.
    And again. And again. And again. And again. And again.
    And again. And again. And again. And again. And again. And again. And again. And again.

Let him who can count,
    count;
let him who knows,
    understand;
let him who believes,
    act."

My Content Study Aid

_____
_____
_____
_____
_____
_____
_____
_____
_____
_____

The Call of The Lord

"I,
   The Lord,
      will go before My people that they may follow The Shepherd of The Flock.

   The sheep will hear My call.

The Call of The Lord will echo in the valleys of The Earth;
          will roll across the plains of The Earth;
          will ascend from the mountains of The Earth.

The Call of The Lord will raise the dead from their graves,
          clothes The Freewill of man,
          will not lift the soul of man,
          prepares man to stand in the courts on high.

The Call of The Lord is final:
          is definite;
          is joyful.

The Call of The Lord is that for which those who serve in Heaven wait.

The Call of The Lord plumbs the oceans of The Earth,
          the seas of The Earth,
          the waters of The Earth.

The Call of The Lord is to the bones of the dead,
          is to the bones of man,
          is heard by the bones of man,
          is spoken for the bones of man.

The Call of The Lord leaves the ashes where they lie.

   For The Temple of The Lord shall not be destroyed by fire,
      The Temple of The Lord that therein dwelt the spirit and freewill of men.

   For The Temple of The Lord,
          when clothed in righteousness,
          shall again be indwelt by man.

   For the Temple of The Lord,
          when judged,
          may again be indwelt by men.

   For the Temple of The Lord may be needed again by man.

I,
   The Lord,
      am doing The Will of The Father.

I,
> The Lord,
>> am commissioning The Spirit afresh.

I,
> The Lord,
>> know The Freewill of God.

I,
> The Lord,
>> know The Freewill of man.

I,
> The Lord,
>> know The Freewill of all creation.

Now,
> The Lord caused His people to turn from their evil ways:
>> by hearing of The Word—
>>> as taught by the servants of The Lord;
>> through understanding of The Word—
>>> as proclaimed by the servants of The Lord;
>> by enacting of The Word—
>>> as witnessed by the servants of The Lord.

The evil ways of Lucifer were manifest in the lives of those who did not know The Lord;
> were evident in the lives of those who did not know The Lord;
> were displayed in the lives of those who did not know The Lord;
> were full-grown in the lives of those who did not know The Lord;
> were recognized in the lives of those who did not know The Lord.

The evil ways of Lucifer were rebuked by The Lord,
> were reviled by The Lord,
> were condemned by The Lord,
> were atoned by The Lord,
> were forbidden to the people of The Lord.

The people did not care,
> would not listen,
> have not heard.

The people now are called,
> by The Spirit,
>> to renounce their sinful ways.

The people now must come on bended knee before The Lord.

> The bended knee may still save man from the wrath of God,
>> shall show man's penitence to God,
>> shall save The Loved of God.

The Loved of God must now repent before The Banquet of The Lord,
>> must now recant the treasures of their lives,
>> must now increase their treasuries in Heaven.

> The treasuries of Heaven will not decrease,
>> store the eternal wealth of man.

> The wealth of man cannot come from the wealth of Lucifer.

> The wealth of man must be stored by man,
>> must be claimed by man.

Man must not build the wealth of Lucifer,
> must not command the servants of Lucifer,
> must not approve the deeds of Lucifer,
> must not emulate the works of Lucifer,
> must not worship Lucifer."

My Content Study Aid

The Fate of The Damned

"Those who worship Lucifer are damned.

The people of The Earth that follow the ways of Lucifer are damned.

    Damnation is the inheritance of the servants of
                The Antichrist,
                The Prince of Darkness,
                The Destroyer of the spirit of man,
                The Deceiver,
                      Lucifer the fallen angel.

The fate of the damned is known to God and now revealed,
                        in part,
                        to man.

The fate of the damned awaits all those who do not love The Lord,
        is determined after the presentation of the records,
        may be tempered by mercy and by law,
        may not be pleaded.

The fate of the damned is fellowship with sin;
            denouncing of man;
            death of man's spirit;
            the rewards of Lucifer;
            The Fires of Hell.

The damned will not glory in their fate,
        will not boast of their fate,
        will not bear witness of their fate.

The damned will scream and not find comfort,
        will hiss and not find love,
        will screech and not find mercy.

The damned of man may not ever enter the courts of praise."

My Content Study Aid

_____

_____

_____

_____

_____

The Chariot of The Lord

"When The Lord had surveyed His Kingdom,
    He raised His hand and blessed all those who were upon their knees
                      for their voices,
                     calling,
                       were heard.

Then The Lord called His chariot and the four living creatures,
         those who guard The Throne of Grace,
         those who would challenge all those who would
              enter from the four corners of The Earth,
         those who strike fear into the hearts of the unjust,
            arose and accompanied The Lord.

The chariot of The Lord,
    dressed in the splendour of the throne,
    dressed in the opulence of love,
    dressed in the splendour of creation,
         arose to greet The Lord.

The chariot of The Lord—
    The Loved of The Lord,
    The Servants of The Lord,
    The Worshippers of The Lord—
         will carry The Lord upon their praises,
         will carry The Lord with their love,
         will carry The Lord along the way.

Prepare the way of The Lord.*

Prepare the way of The Lord.

Prepare the way of The Lord.

The way of The Lord will now be prepared by the people of The Lord for the coming of
                              The Lord.

Prepare the way of The Lord.*

Prepare the way of The Lord.

Prepare the way of The Lord.

The way of The Lord shall recognize The Spirit,
            uplift The Son and exalt The Father.

The way of The Lord shall not come down.

The way of The Lord shall encircle.

The way of The Lord shall vanquish.

Prepare the way of The Lord.*

Prepare the way of The Lord.

Prepare the way of The Lord.

Those who maintain the way of The Lord will be blessed by God,
> who recognize the way of The Lord will be welcomed by God,
> who acclaim the way of The Lord will be uplifted by God.

Those who despise the way of The Lord are not known by God."

Scribal Note: *Refer* The Bible (NKJV) Luke 3:4-6, Isaiah 40:3-5.
Luke 3:4-6
4 as it is written in the book of The Words of Isaiah the prophet, saying: "The voice of one crying in the wilderness: 'Prepare the way of the LORD; Make His paths straight. 5 Every valley shall be filled And every mountain and hill brought low; The crooked places shall be made straight And the rough ways smooth; 6 And all flesh shall see the salvation of God.' "

Isaiah 40:3-5.
3 The voice of one crying in the wilderness: "Prepare the way of the LORD; Make straight in the desert A highway for our God. 4 Every valley shall be exalted And every mountain and hill brought low; The crooked places shall be made straight And the rough places smooth; 5 The glory of the LORD shall be revealed, And all flesh shall see [it] together; For the mouth of the LORD has spoken."

My Content Study Aid

_____
_____
_____
_____
_____
_____
_____
_____
_____
_____
_____
_____
_____

The Four Living Creatures

"The Four Living Creatures who were in the throne room will then precede The Lord,
fulfilling duties so and then assigned.

The four living creatures are numbered by The Lord.

The four living creatures have the faces of The Lord,
have the signs of The Lord.

The four living creatures are the signals of The Lord,
are numbered by the quadrants of The Lord.

The quadrant of one,
emblazoned with the numeral on its flank,
is the vanguard of those who go before.

The quadrant of one foretells,
rebukes,
relates,
knows.

The quadrant of two,
emblazoned with the numeral on its shoulder,
evaluates all things for those who now are there.

The quadrant of two decides,
confirms,
seals,
knows.

The quadrant of three,
emblazoned with the numeral on its chest,
condones the deeds for those now there,
of quadrants one and two.

The quadrant of three verifies,
examines,
knows.

The quadrant of four,
emblazoned with the numeral on its forehead,
adjusts the way of those who will process.

The quadrant of four determines,
confirms,
is.

The quadrant numbered four affirms,

> re-affirms,
> declines.

The quadrant of four brought the quadrant of one forth;
> brought the quadrant of two to attention and the quadrant of three
>> to service.

Let those who reason,
> know;
let those who know,
> respect;
let those who respect,
> complete.

The living creatures are released by The Lord.

The living creatures will not settle,
> will not come together,
> will not stop,
> will come when called.

The living creatures are known one to another,
> move in unison,
> bow before,
> gather in.

The living creatures respond to love,
> protect,
> garnish,
> convince.

   Mighty are the ways of the living creatures.

The living creatures are aware of a new way traversed by the Sun."

My Content Study Aid

_____
_____
_____
_____
_____
_____
_____
_____

The Lord Will Come

"The Lord will come for those He loves—
                      the loved of The Lord,
                      the children of man.

The Lord will come according to The Word,
      will come when commissioned by The Father.

The Father now commissions.

The Lord now so prepares.

The Lord surveys His Kingdom;
                      blesses,
                      listens,
                      calls.

Mighty were the ways of The Lord;
      are the ways of The Lord;
      will be the ways of The Lord.

Majestic will be the way of The Lord.

Glorious will be the way of The Lord.

Triumphant will be the way of The Lord.

In triumph will The Lord come for His Bride,
                      select His Bride,
                      receive His Bride.

The Bride of The Lord shall know no fear,
                      shall conquer sin,
                      shall renovate the courts.

The Bride of The Lord shall hold the reins;
                      shall guide the lost;
                      shall lead the responders.

Responsible is The Bride of The Lord for—
                      recovery of sight among the blind,
                      recovery of hearing among the deaf,
                      recovery of speech among the mute.

When recovery is complete all shall rejoice,
                      the gates are closed,
                      torment shall commence.

Torment is for the blind,
                the deaf,

> the mute—
> those that did not travel through the gate.

The strong man shall not travel through the gate.

The cohorts shall not travel through the gate.

The legions shall not travel through the gate.

Travelling through the gate is at The Will of The Lord,
> prevents return,
> denies history,
> uplifts the soul."

My Content Study Aid

The Gate To Life

"The gate to life is difficult to find for those who know not where to search,
        is impossible to open for those who do not hold the key,
        remains shut to those who may not pass.

  For those who know the way the gate to life swings open wide,
           the gate to life presents itself,
           the gate to life will never close.

The closing of the gate cancels sin,
        locks in sin,
        determines sin.

Those who love The Lord will not be at the closing of the gate.

  The closing of the gate shall presage the closing of The Freewill.

  The freewill is closed when learning stops,
        when light is gone,
        when darkness reigns.

  The freewill is closed where joy is not,
        where confusion reigns,
        where all is lost.

  Suffer not The Freewill to be closed.

  Close not The Freewill of man.

  The freewill of man do not close.

  Closing of The Freewill presages The Death numbered by Two.

  The Death of Two affects The Freewill of man,
        affects the spirit of man,
        affects the company of man,
        outweighs The Death of One.

  The Freewill of man should avoid The Death of Two.

  The Freewill of man can now avoid The Death of Two.

  The Freewill of man by seeing,
        listening,
        hearing,
        doing,
            can avoid The Death of Two.

  The Freewill of man that seeks and finds will avoid The Death of Two.

  The Death numbered by Three is final.

The Death of Three is beyond redemption.

The Death of Three cancels all.

Woe to any man subject to the Death of Three.

The Death of Three outweighs all those that go before.

There is no gate that opens inwards from The Death of Three.

When The Lord heard the praises of His people,
    those borne to the heavens by the chariot of fervency,
        of enthusiasm,
        of endeavour,
    then The Lord recognized the voices of His people.

The Lord will recognize the voice of His people—
    those who know His Name;
    those saved by grace;
    those redeemed from the fall;
    those hallowed by His Name;
    those committed by The Father;
    those cared for by the angels;

    those uplifted by The Spirit;
    those to be welcomed by The Son;
    those to be installed by The Son;
    those to be seated with The Son;
    those to reign with The Son;
    those to know eternity;
    those who not fear death.

The Lord beckons,
    and these,
        The Loved of The Lord—
            come running to the seat of their salvation,
            are welcomed to their Glory,
            rejoice with The Spirit in their Inheritance."

My Content Study Aid

_____
_____
_____
_____
_____
_____

The Ways of The Spirit

"O,
    rejoice in The Spirit,
    rejoice with The Spirit,
    rejoice for The Spirit.

The Spirit rejoices with the spirit of man in the courts on high,
        with man at the destiny of man,
        when man is called.

The Spirit,
The Holy Spirit,
The Comforter,
    rejoices when man hears The Call of God;
        hears the whisper of his spirit;
        hears the fullness of The Word;
            for then changes the destiny of man.

The Spirit greets;
The Spirit embraces;
The Spirit enfolds;
The Spirit endows;
The Spirit affirms;
The Spirit lauds;
The Spirit enacts;
The Spirit leads.

The Spirit commends;
The Spirit directs;
The Spirit contacts;
The Spirit delivers;
The Spirit reports;
The Spirit records;
The Spirit notifies.

The Spirit evaluates;
The Spirit approves;
The Spirit convinces;
The Spirit convicts;
The Spirit denotes;
The Spirit inspires;
The Spirit revokes;
The Spirit condemns.

The Spirit uplifts.

The Spirit reveals.

The Spirit rejoices.

>Mighty are the ways of The Spirit,
>>are the deeds of The Spirit,
>>are the celebrations of The Spirit.

>The celebrations of The Spirit are directed by The Lord;
>>>are consummated by The Lord;
>>>are in character with The Lord.

The Spirit celebrates when the love of man is heard.

The Spirit celebrates when man,
>>around The Banquet of The Lord,
>>is gathered.

The Spirit celebrates when man's spirit is acknowledged by man's Freewill;
>when man's spirit subjects man's soul;
>when man's soul is loosed from Lucifer;
>when the living creatures numbered by four are loosed;
>when man is loosed from the bondage of his soul.

The Spirit welcomes the soul of man when it is renewed,
>>the spirit of man when accompanied by The Freewill,
>>The Temple of man when it is complete.

The Spirit cleaves the soul of man at the passing of the flesh,
>cleaves that man may be redeemed,
>cleaves that Lucifer may not control The Freewill of man,
>cleaves that The Throne Rooms remain The Sanctuary of God.

>The Sanctuary of God is held sacred to the trust.

>The Sanctuary of God is for The Company of God—
>>>those called by the name of The Lord—
>>>those called by the authority of The Father—
>>>those called by the sovereign act of The Sovereign God.

>The Sanctuary of God will prevail throughout eternity.

The Spirit cleanses the soul of man at the passing of the flesh.

The Spirit,
>at the passing of the flesh,
>>>surveys the soul of man;
>>>evaluates the soul of man;
>>>records the soul of man in The Book of Life.

The soul of man,
>at the passing of the flesh,

at the death of the flesh,
at the end of man's life upon The Earth,
>is received by The Soul of God."

My Content Study Aid

The Soul of God

"The Soul of God refines;
    restores;
    renews.

The Soul of God burnishes the soul of man.

The Soul of God detects the soul of man,
    regenerates the soul of man,
     announces the soul of man when so prepared to serve.

 The soul of man shall serve in The Temple of The Spirit or in The Fires of Hell.

Then The Lord Sovereign God opened the eyes of His people,
    opened the ears of His people,
    opened the mouths of His people.

His people saw,
  heard and prayed.

 Great were their prayers before The Lord,
    The Sovereign God of Creation.

The prayers of His people were like incense in the nostrils of The Lord.

The prayers of His people,
    spoken in love,
    anointed by The Spirit,
    carried by the angels,
    swept through the throne rooms of Heaven.

 They left a trail of love that the angels could follow;
     could follow all the way to The Earth;
     could follow to all those who cried to The Lord.

The angels plied to and fro with steadfastness and zeal;
  plied with love and trepidation;
  plied in trust and in service:
     for,
     of,
    and to,
     all those who cried to The Lord,
       their Sovereign God."

The Prayers of The Faithful

"The prayers of The Faithful support the thrones of Heaven.

> For their prayers cause the strongholds of Lucifer to crumble;
> > the strongholds of Lucifer to wither;
> > the strongholds of Lucifer to bow before The Lord.

> The strongholds of Lucifer are wrecked by the prayers of The Faithful.

The prayers of The Faithful will proceed from the mouths of those who love The Lord;
> > of those who serve The Lord;
> > of those who worship The Lord.

The prayers of The Faithful build The Book of Life,
> > are therein recorded,
> > are thereby revealed."

My Content Study Aid

The Prayers of The Just and Unjust

"The prayers of the just do not stand,
                are not recorded in The Book of Life,
                have no authority before The Lord.

The prayers of the just,
                those who do not know The Lord,
                waste their breath with prayer.

The prayers of the just are not heard by the angels.

For when the just come before The Lord in prayer they cloak themselves with
                              their own righteousness,
                              their own justification.

The just are not justified before The Lord,
                will not be justified before The Lord,
                shall not be justified before The Lord.

The just should find the gate that justifies all those that enter through.

The prayers of the unjust are first heard as cries of repentance to The Throne of Grace.

The prayers of the unjust are then recorded,
                are then answered,
                are then celebrated.

The repentant prayers of the unjust justify in Faith,
                acknowledge in brokenness and accept in humbleness.

The unjust are then justified in the sight of The Lord."

My Content Study Aid

_____
_____
_____
_____
_____
_____
_____
_____

The Prayers of The Justified

"Arise,
    The Justified of The Lord,
        arise.

The prayers of The Justified shout to The Lord;
        appeal to The Lord;
        seek The Lord.

The prayers of The Justified continue,
        develop,
        are in Faith.
  In Faith,
  and in love,
  are the prayers of The Justified rendered to the heavens.

The prayers of the damned are too late,
        shall not avail,
        are heard by Lucifer.

The prayers of the damned uttered in anguish,
        rejected in justice,
        condemned without mercy,
        feed The Flames of Hell.

  Woe to those who utter the prayers of the damned."

My Content Study Aid

_____
_____
_____
_____
_____
_____
_____
_____
_____
_____

The Prayers of the Indwelt

"The prayers of those indwelt by The Spirit have access to the thrones.

The prayers of those indwelt are recorded in The Record of The Son.

The prayers of those indwelt,
          transmitted by the angels,
          approved by The Spirit,
          received by the thrones,
          acknowledged by The Son,
          give thanks and praise and worship to and for The Son,
                                            The Risen Christ.

The prayers of those indwelt reverberate in Heaven,
          echo in the halls,
          carry through the courts.

The prayers of those indwelt as uttered by the flesh are answered according to the flesh,
          by the spirit are answered according to The Spirit.

The prayers of those indwelt know The Spirit's working;
          know The Spirit's leading;
          know The Spirit's presence.

Come,
    all those indwelt,
        before The Throne of Grace.

Come,
    all those indwelt,
        into the courts of praise.

Come,
    all those indwelt,
        and stand before your fellow man.

Come and speak,
 come and testify,
 come and welcome—
        to those that would hear,
        to those that would receive—
              those that would come.

Come and rejoice at the salvation of man;
        at the redemption of man;
        at the destiny of man.

Come and worship The Lord,

> The Spirit,
> The Father.

Come and worship The God of Israel,
> The God of The Patriarchs,
> The God of The Word,
> The God of Eternity,
> The God of Creation,
> The God of man,
> The God of Isaac,

> The God of Jacob,
> The God of Abraham,
> The God of Melchizedek,
> The God of Moses,
> The God of David,
> The God of Enoch,
> The God of Isaiah:

> The God of Revelation.

Come,
> now,
>> on bended knee into the presence of your God.

Know your God.

Know your God.

Know your God.

> Your God calls.

> Your God requires all those who love The Lord to serve The Lord.

Prepare the way of The Lord.

Prepare the way of The Lord.

Prepare the way of The Lord.

The Lord will soon require the prepared way.

> Now is the time to serve your God,
>> to praise your God,
>> to worship your God.

> Seek your God while judgement is with-held,
>> while The Spirit moves,
>> while the seat of mercy holds.

> Now is the time to seek your God while He may still be discovered,
>> to be drawn to God while He still calls.

Hear The Call of The Lord,
> of The Spirit,
>> from The Father.

Soon the call will be silenced,
> the heavens will shut,
>> man's destiny will be determined.

Come now with renewed Faith;
> with renewed Freewill;
>> with recommitment to The Lord,
>>> your God.

For majestic are the ways of The Lord;
in justice and mercy does The Lord process;
in love and obedience does The Lord progress.

Mighty is the way of The Lord.

Prepare for the way of The Lord.

Wait on the way of The Lord.

See the way of The Lord.

The way of The Lord is coming.

Come and prepare at The Banquet of The Lord,
> The House of The Lord,
> The Temple of The Lord,
> The Dwelling-place of The Lord,
> with The Spirit.

Come.

Come.

Come.

God calls;
> man waits.

God calls;
> man declines.

God calls;
> man suffers.

God is silent;
> man screams.

God is silent;
> man searches.

God is silent;
> man panics.

Come,
> now,
> before the closing of the gate.

Come,
> now,
> while the sun shines.

Come,
> now,
> while it is today.

Come to The Lord,
 come with The Spirit,
 come before The Father.

Come.

Come.

Come.

> Hear The Call of The Lord,
>> all corners of The Earth.
>
> Accept The Call of The Lord,
>> all corners of The Earth.

Come before The Lord with thanksgiving,
> rejoicing,
> exalting.

> Repent of the ways of man.
>
> Acknowledge the ways of God.

Come,
> discover your God while He may yet be found."

My Content Study Aid

_____
_____
_____
_____
_____
_____
_____

The Destiny of Lucifer

"And so it was,
    that Lucifer,
        having been created in the image of God,
           was set in the heavenly places to rule with God.

Lucifer grew in knowledge and in understanding,
    in authority and in influence,
    in stature and in perception.

Lucifer attained his destiny.

Lucifer wanted more.

Lucifer encouraged the created beings,
    the angels,
        to change allegiance.

Lucifer promised what he could not keep,
    what he could not do,
    what he could not deliver to those,
        his servants,
        in rebellion.
        They believed him.
        They trusted him.
        They followed him.

Then The Lord Sovereign God,
    the Almighty,
    The Holy One of Israel surveyed all of His creation—
            and the cause of dissent and the result of dissent were torn
            from the heavenly places where they had been set by God.

    All those in dissent,
        those that did not agree,
        those that did not bow,
        those that did not acknowledge were despatched to another realm that
            they may be company one to another.

Lucifer challenged God.
    challenged the righteousness of the creation of God.

God accepted the challenge from His creation.

Lucifer,
    His creation,
        was given dominion over The Earth for a time.

Lucifer was permitted to attempt to thwart the plans of God for The Earth.

Lucifer did not know the plans of God,
    did not see The Book of Life,
    shall not see The Book of Life.

Now Lucifer and those who dissented attempt to steer man away from God,
        attempt to prevent man's attainment of his destiny,
        attempt to prevent God's walk with man.

And Lucifer's success is according to the agency of man—
        a gift of God,
        that man may choose in whom he will trust,
            whom he will believe,
            to whom he will respond.

And God has made himself known to His creation and has provided a way out
        from disobedience;
    that man,
    His creation,
    may again walk with God and
        recover from the fall from
        grace instigated by Lucifer.

And Lucifer lures The Freewill of men with the souls of men.

    Lucifer lures and God forbids,
        seizes and God records,
        claims and God offers.

    Lucifer may not overcome the agency of man.

Man remains free to turn from Lucifer until the death of the flesh.

Lucifer is the enemy of man.

Lucifer knows the soul of man,
    has access to the soul of man,
    influences the soul of man.

    Beware of the soul of man.

    The soul of man leads man to destruction.

    Let The Freewill of man not be subject to the soul of man.

Then Lucifer used immorality,
        depravity,
        greed,
        lust,
        envy to destroy The Temple of the flesh.

Then Lucifer used disobedience,
>> guilt,
>> remorse,
>> insanity to imprison The Freewill of man.

Then Lucifer used lies,
>> deceit,
>> and all forms of iniquity,
>> to destroy the spirit of man.

And Lucifer laughed at those who accepted the wages of sin—
>> for he knew their destiny.

>> Beware of the wages of sin.

>> The wages of sin are no treasure,
>>> may not be redeemed,
>>> entail the destruction of man.

>> Accept not the wages of sin.

>> Do not touch the wages of sin.

>> Bank not the wages of sin.

>> Shy from The Paymaster of Sin,
>>> The Banker of Men's Souls,
>>> The Accountant of Hell.

Lucifer is now dominant in The Freewill of men.

Lucifer now has captured the ways of men,
>> rejoices at his success,
>> believes he cannot lose,
>> looks to the day of account.

Now,
> in accord with The Book of Life,
>> The Spirit,
>> The Holy Spirit,
>> The Holy Messenger,
>> The Holy Instigator,
>>> is released afresh upon The Earth.

The Spirit will now test the agency of man.

The Spirit will now reclaim the living from the dead,
>> those in whom the conscience lives,
>> all those who comprehend the reality of God.

Let those who read,
> understand.

Let those who understand,
> decide.

Let those who decide,
> be so judged."

My Content Study Aid

The Prayer of The Lord

"Our Father,
      The Beloved of His Children,
      Glorify Your Name in all the heavens and over all The Earth.

May Your Thrones be adorned throughout eternity according to Your Will.

Let The Temples of The Spirit be so prepared for those who love The Lord.
Continue to let The Spirit dwell in the hearts of man this day.
Listen to The Son as He pleads in mercy before The Throne for His sheep.

Accept those who stand before You,
            as ordained and dressed,
           in The Blood of The Lamb.

Receive all honour,
      praise and worship that issue from our lips—
      that You may be exalted above all,
            O Father,
            throughout time."

My Content Study Aid

Chapter 7: The Ordaining of The Servants

The Spirit Structures

"The Spirit loves The Son,
    loves The Father,
    loves creation.

The Spirit moves amongst the creation of The Lord,
    witnesses the creation of The Lord,
    knows the creation of The Lord,
    speaks to the creation of The Lord.

The Spirit records the creation of The Lord,
    records the deeds of creation in The Book of Life for The Son as The Record of The Son,
    records the deeds of man in The Book of Life for The Son as The Record of The Son.

The Spirit loves man.

The Spirit serves The Father,
    The Son,
    and man.

The Spirit knows the end of times,
    the coming of The Lord is near,
    The Father has now commissioned The Son.

The Spirit now goes forth.

The Spirit now marshals the powers of Heaven to assist,
    assembles the throngs,
    arrays the soldiers of The Lord.

The Spirit now is clothed with power,
    is clothed with urgency,
    is clothed with the mantle of The Lord.

The Spirit now evaluates The Saints on Earth.

The Spirit will pass over,
    will call up,
    will assemble,
    will teach,
    will guide.

The Spirit will reveal the plans of God to man:

the plans of God now necessary to defeat the prince of darkness.

The plans of God will be done in boldness of The Spirit,
> will come forth to head a mighty army,
> will not be for the weak.

The plans of God are for those now to be prepared.

Those now to be prepared will go through,
> will not wilt,
> will endure,
> will survive.

The Spirit will safeguard the soldiers of The Cross,
> will record the soldiers of The Cross,
> will support the soldiers of The Cross."

My Content Study Aid

The Banner of The Cross

"The Spirit will uplift The Banner of The Cross,
    will receive The Banner of The Cross,
    will recognize The Banner of The Cross.

    Search for The Banner of The Cross.

    Lift high The Banner of The Cross.

    Protect The Banner of The Cross.

The Banner of The Cross will mark the way of The Lord.

    Unfurl The Banner of The Cross.

    Fly The Banner of The Cross.

    Honour The Banner of The Cross.

Mighty will be The Banner of The Cross before the nations of The Earth,
        over the oceans of The Earth,
        over all The Earth and sea and sky.

Prepare for The Banner of The Cross.

The Spirit will prepare the people of The Lord to receive The Banner of The Cross.

The Spirit now brings forth The Banner of The Cross.

    Seek for The Banner of The Cross.

    Be covered by The Banner of The Cross.

The Banner of The Cross will protect the people of The Lord,
    will identify the people of The Lord.

    Woe to those not covered by The Banner of The Cross at the coming of The Lord.

The Spirit speaks to all the people of The Lord.

    Be protected by The Banner of The Cross;
        The Banner of The Son;
        The Banner of the Blood;
        The Banner for all corners of The Earth.

Let those who know The Banner,
        obtain it.

Let those who obtain it,
        fly it.

Let those who fly it,
        know protection.

The weapon marked with a 'V' is soon to be placed in the throne room for the angel.

Let him who reads,
        comprehend.

Let him who hears,
        read.

Let him who doubts,
        ignore.

Let him who believes,
        act."

My Content Study Aid

_____
_____
_____
_____
_____
_____
_____
_____
_____
_____
_____
_____
_____
_____
_____
_____
_____
_____
_____
_____
_____
_____
_____

The Record of The Spirit

"Mighty are the ways of The Living Creatures.

The Spirit records the works of Lucifer.

The Spirit records the actions of the demons,
> records all deeds of sin,
> records all thoughts of sin,
> records all knowledge of sin.

Disobedience to God is recorded by The Spirit,
> is recorded in The Spirit,
>> for The Spirit.

The Spirit shall so testify if called.

The testimony of The Spirit is given in full,
> may not be stopped once started.

The testimony of The Spirit is truth,
> is impartial,
> is believed.

The Record of The Spirit includes the spirit of man,
> condemns Lucifer.

The Record of The Spirit contains the activities of the soul of man:
> the deeds,
> the thoughts,
> the motives that bore upon The Freewill.

> The reasoning of The Freewill,
> the attacks on The Freewill,
> the support of The Freewill:
>> all are known and kept within The Record of The Spirit.

The Record of The Spirit kept within man's lifetime of the flesh will not prevail.

The Record of the flesh of man will die when The Temple of The Spirit is raised up,
> will die with the death of man's spirit.

The Record of The Spirit may continue in The Temple of The Spirit.

> Prepare now for the Temple of The Spirit,
>> for the presence of The Spirit,
>> for the indwelling of The Spirit.

> Walk not in the ways of the flesh.

> For the ways of the flesh do not uplift The Freewill,

>   do not uplift the spirit,
>   do not uplift the condition of man.
>
> Walk,
> rather,
> in the ways of The Spirit each day;
> for therein lies the conquest of the soul,
>   the extension of The Freewill,
>   the walk with God.
>
> God spoke to His people by the voice of the prophet,
>   by the writings of the prophet,
>   by the teachings of the prophet.
>
> God spoke to His people that they may not be lost,
>   that they may be prepared,
>   that they may rejoice in the knowledge of His love."

My Content Study Aid

The Faith of The People

"And The Faith of the people was tried.

And The Faith of the people was tested.

And The Faith of the people failed.

And The Faith of the people was restored.

The Faith of the people was renewed by the moving of The Spirit.

The Faith of the people will prevail,
    will suffice,
    will justify—
        all those who would know The Lord.

  For Faith is the harbinger of miracles;
    is the harbinger of hope;
    is the harbinger of eternal life.

Faith initiates the walk with God;
  maintains the walk with God;
  improves the walk with God.

Faith comes to The Freewill of man at the awakening of man's spirit,
      when The Call of God is heard within man's soul,
      when answering The Call of God.

    When Faith comes,
        doubts leave;
   when Faith comes,
        joy enters:
   when Faith comes,
        The Spirit moves;
   when Faith comes,
        peace comes;
   when Faith comes,
        sin retreats;
   when Faith comes,
        the soul pouts;
   when Faith comes,
        angels are assigned;
   when Faith comes,
        The Book of Life is entered.

    When Faith comes,
        The Son rejoices with The Father and The Spirit.

At the coming of Faith the soul calls for help,
> the soul requests assistance,
> the soul receives according to the call.

Beware of the call of the soul of man.

Do not heed the soul of man.

Do not let Faith die.

For when Faith dies The Freewill of man is damaged by the soul,
> > man's spirit retreats and awaits another day,
> > the heavens grieve and hope is lost.

Faith precedes service.

Faith precedes love.

Faith precedes knowledge.

Faith precedes understanding.

Faith precedes the invitation to The Banquet of The Lord.

Faith precedes the attainment of man's destiny.

Let he who has Faith,
> learn:

let he who has Faith,
> serve;

let he who has Faith,
> go."

My Content Study Aid

_____
_____
_____
_____
_____
_____
_____
_____
_____
_____
_____
_____
_____

The Triumvirate of God

"Now the heavens would disclose their presence to all of man.

The heavens would disclose their majesty on high,
                the regality of The Son,
                the sanctity of The Father,
                and the repose of The Spirit.

The regality of The Son was decreed by The Father,
                was maintained by The Father,
                was determined by The Father.

The regality of The Son comes from The Throne of Grace.

The Son sits on The Throne of Grace.

The Son shall remain on The Throne of Grace.

The Son creates The Temple of The Spirit,
            The Temple of The Lord,
            The Temple of Grace.
            Beautiful is The Temple,
            welcoming is The Temple,
            loving is The Temple.

The Son reviews the flesh lives of those who claim to know The Lord.

The Son promotes before The Father all those who know The Lord.

The Father hears The Record of The Spirit and of The Son.

The Father bequeaths to the heirs according to The Word,
                according to His Will,
                according to the contents of The Book of Life.

The heirs may then claim their promises,
        may then claim their treasures,
        may then claim their places so reserved.

The Father,
    in The Sanctuary of God,
    brought before the thrones all those whom The Son had rejected:
                all those who falsely claimed,
                all those who did not claim,
                all those who would not claim,
                all those who could not claim.

There,
    before The Father on The Throne of White,

The Book of Life was opened and the Record of The Son was read.

There,
> before The Father on The Throne of White,
> The Record of The Spirit was available to those who asked that it be told.

There,
> before The Father on The Throne of White,
> the record of the angels was there shown.

All those seated on the thrones then made judgement on those not known before
> The Lord,
> according to The Records,
> and to the testimony of man.

> They then were brought before The Father and the presence of The Son.

> The Spirit told the judgement incurred by that flesh life.

> The mercy of The Son was seen in love.

> The judgement of The Father was seen as just.

> The punishment commenced according to the law.

> The fate of those so judged was not spoken of again.

> The fate of those condemned was as written in The Word and their names were no longer in The Book of Life.

The Spirit rests within the sanctuary of God.

The Spirit has the seal of God,
> uses the seal of God,
> brings the seal of God.

> Be sealed with the seal of The Spirit.

> Be sealed with the seal by The Spirit.

> Be sealed with the seal for the spirit.

The spirit of man requires the seal of The Spirit.

> Do not deny the seal of The Spirit.

> Do not deny the seal of God.

> Do not deny the imprint of Heaven on The Freewill of man.

The Spirit has the scroll of The Lord and the scroll of The Father.

The Spirit actions what is written on the scrolls.

Loving and just are what are numbered on the scrolls.

The scrolls written in the heavens,

    carried by the angels,
    are actioned on The Earth through The Spirit.

The Son seeks,
 The Father knows,
  The Spirit acts.

Mighty are The Ways of God;
awe full are The Ways of God;
regal are The Ways of God.

The Ways of God shall endure.

    The death of the flesh is of man.

    The death of the flesh is of woman.

    The death of the flesh is the inheritance of Lucifer.

    The death of the spirit is the work of Lucifer.

    Let not man's spirit die.

All those who overcome Lucifer in their flesh lives will overcome the death of the flesh.

    For those who overcome,
            there is no fear;
  for those who overcome,
            there is no punishment;
  for those who overcome,
            the heavens await.

        Overcome The Devil.

        Overcome The Prince of Darkness.

        Overcome Beelzebub.

        Overcome Satan.

        Overcome The Captor of the souls.

        Overcome The Antichrist.

        Overcome Lucifer.

        Overcome The Fallen One.

    For those who overcome,
            a crown awaits in The Kingdom of The Lord.

    The Freewill of man must be redeemed.

    When The Freewill of man receives The Spirit,
            knows The Spirit,
            dwells with The Spirit then the death of the flesh
                        can cause no harm,
                        can cause no fear,

> can cause no loss.

Then welcome—
> the death of the flesh.

For those who do not seek,
> who do not find,
> who do not know—
>> the death of the flesh is to be feared.

Then God surveyed The Earth and disliked much of what He saw;
> for many nations built images of God;
> put them in high places and worshipped them.

> And The Sovereign God spread out His hand again
> over all the nations that worshipped those idols,
> and led them to a place of destruction for they
> had no place among the families of God.

The nations that loved The Lord grew in numbers and their praises were as incense in the
> nostrils of The Lord as they prospered.

Angels from Heaven were sent to all corners of The Earth to see the works of men;
> and men chosen by God communed with angels
> as The Glory of The Lord filled their hearts.

Then The Lord God Almighty spoke to the elements:
> and all those enthroned in the universe were amazed:
> at the authority displayed before them.

Those at the footstools of the thrones praised The Lamb of God.

The angels travelled throughout The Earth carrying the news:
> that now before the nations would be displayed The Lamb of God—
> so that all mankind may know their Redeemer,
>> The Messiah of the Jews,
> sacrificed in love for the peoples of The Earth.

The Lord Sovereign God wept.

> For He knew the fate of The Lamb before He was sent to His chosen people,
> and He knew that they would kill Him,
> and He knew that the time was short for the salvation of the nations,
> and He knew that His vineyard was now being tended by His Son,
> The Chosen One from the beginning who had tended and planted
>> The garden of The Lord.

Now it came to pass that The Lord wept at the wickedness of the nations,
> for He saw how the hearts of the people had hardened,
> and led them to persecute the pure in heart,
>> the anointed of The Lord:

> those ordained from before the foundations of The Earth:
> > to minister to the people with The Glory of The Lord.

So the loved of The Lord sang their praises to the kings of The Earth:
> and few there were who remained holy before The Lord.

The Lord regarded His people and His heart was saddened at what He saw;
> for spread before Him was the offerings from idols;
> > and the stench of the unclean things of
> > > The Earth pervaded the realms of Heaven.

The Sovereign Lord regarded The Earth,
> and saw the iniquity of those He had placed in authority—
> > over the peoples of the nations:
> and His heart broke when He saw how the leaders of the nations,
> > ordained by Him,
> > > had destroyed The Faith of the people:
> > > > by their behaviour before The Lord.

Now,
> I,
> > The Sovereign Lord God,
> > > decree that as the heavens and The Earth are My creation—
> > > > so shall the peoples,
> > > > > and the creatures of My creation bow before Me.

No longer shall I suffer My anointed to be hammered by Lucifer.

For from this time on I shall lift up My anointed servants,
> and they shall carry My Banner before them—
> > as they go forth across the nations preaching good-will,
> > > peace and love to those who know My Name.

My servants shall speak with fire,
> and the wrath of God shall be on their lips,
> and the love of God shall be in their hearts.

And the majesty of God shall be displayed before His creation—
> so that the peoples of all The Earth shall be aware
> > of the sacrifice of His Son:
> > > that those who hear the voice of The Lord may be
> > > > called the sons and daughters of God.

My servants shall minister in power and with authority from on high so
> that The Lord may be Glorified.

And this is how they shall be recognised:
> they shall come ministering in all the gifts of The
> > Glory of The Risen King;
> they shall praise and honour The Name of The Risen King—

> The Lamb,
> The Lord,
> The Christ,
> The Saviour to all mankind,
> The Alpha and The Omega—
> > and Him alone.

> Mighty shall be their endeavours for in The Name of The Risen King
> > they shall cast out demons,
> > they shall bless the people,
> > they shall heal the sick,
> > they shall lay waste the works of Lucifer,
> > they shall reveal The Word of The Lamb,
> > > and The Glory of The Lord shall confirm
> > > > My Word in the hearts of men.

> My servants shall humble themselves before The Lord,
> > and they shall have kings kneel before them,
> > and they shall go where The Glory of The Lord will lead them.

> Mighty will be their voices—
> > as they minister to the nations of The Earth.

> The hand of The Lord shall direct the harvesting of the nations:
> > > many will hear the voice of The Lord,
> > > many will see the angels of Heaven,
> > > many will smell the incense of The Lord.

> And Lucifer screamed at all the nations—
> > and turned those anointed by The Lord back to their iniquities:
> > save a few who were pure in heart before The Lord.

Then The Blessed of The Lord danced and rejoiced to the music of Heaven.

> For they were instructed in the things of Heaven—
> > and their angels ministered urgently—
> > as they acquired the knowledge to defeat Lucifer
> > > throughout all nations of The Earth.

And those who could see,
> saw;
and those who could hear,
> heard.

And those who knew The Glory of The Lord:
> obeyed the voices of the angels as they defeated Lucifer.

And understanding of The Word was conferred upon all those who were pure in heart.

Then The Lord called a prophet to the nations,

from amongst the islands of the seas,
so that The Word could be spread over all the face of The Earth.

The prophet arose and Lucifer tempted him with many voices that he might subvert the crucifixion of The Lord.

And the prophet was instructed with the things of Heaven—
so that the anointed of The Lord may be blessed as they served throughout the nations—
and ministered with the power and authority of the blood-bought Son of The Living God.

I,
The Lord,
cause this to be written this day.

Change not,
add not,
delete not what The Lord,
your God,
has laid before His people.

For herein is the pathway to Heaven;
herein lies the way of salvation;
herein is The Coming of The Lord."

My Content Study Aid

_____
_____
_____
_____
_____
_____
_____
_____
_____
_____
_____
_____
_____
_____

Appendix—

Tongues of Man	89
Tongues of Demons (2)	91
Revelation 6:1-8 plus Others	92
Horses, Riders, Creatures	93
End-time Summary of God	94
Journaling and Notes (1)	96
Journaling and Notes (2)	97
About the Scribe	98
Epilogue - 'Our GOD Lives'	99
9 End-time Psalms of God	100
or The End-time Homilies of God	
4 End-time Flowers of God	101
Synopses of Flowers of God	101

'This book is as God wanted it for presenting to The World.'

The Scribe
2.12 am 22nd March 2020
Hamilton, NZ.

Tongues of Man

"The tongues of man are voluble and tiring,
                are constructive and teaching,
                are formulating and driving,
                are sequencing and deriving,
                are proclaiming and striving,
                are expanding and thriving.

The tongues of man are circuitous and haphazard,
                are fortuitous and repenting,
                are mischievous and devious.

The tongues of man are the sidesteppers of the truth,
                are the lingerers on lies,
                are the majoring on truths,
                are the hazing of the lies,
                are the broadcasters of the clouded truth,
                are the adopters of the lies.

The tongues of man are the foragers and the hunters of expression,
                are the most loving and the kindest when emotion takes the lead,
                are the most secretive as whisperers and public when in the domain
                                        of proclamations,
                are the most verbal and most restrained of the talkers known to God.

The tongues of man are taxing in forgiveness,
                are lambasting in their anger,
                are accusing to their roots,
                are transfixing in their threats.

The tongues of man jump into the arguments,
                circle the discussions,
                withdraw when wisdom has cause to be displayed.

The tongues of man release without curbing,
                shout without necessity,
                mumble when apologetic.

The tongues of man know the barbs of treachery,
                know the arrows tipped with poison,
                know the lies which generate rebellion.

The tongues of man are circumspect when authorities are present,
                seek approval with compliance,
                build the stories on the rumours when the facts are scarce.

The tongues of man jump on band wagons without a thought,

    stir up trouble for all and sundry,
    mix and stir the pot of inappropriateness:
         for ladling out upon demand.

The tongues of man discern but fail to verify,
    take gossip as the truth,
    spread fear and hurts to the right and left where an audience exists.

The tongues of man often lack sincerity of intent,
    often lack commitment to a script,
    often lack truthfulness when questioned,
    often lack the sense to pause and test the wind.

The tongues of man are heard in contestation,
    are heard when encircled by encouragement,
    are heard when visited with messages deserving of attention.

The tongues of man get man into trouble through the lack of wisdom,
    get man into misunderstandings through the lack of clarity,
    get man into arguments where ignorance is both plentiful
         and widespread.

The tongues of man retreat from the firing lines of innuendos,
     from the firing lines of insults,
     from the firing lines of abrasive conflicts.

The tongues of man are deceptive and powerful,
    can open the alleyways to fisticuffs,
    can result in injuries,
    can result in perjuries,
    can result in strategies of lies,
    can result in the opening of the floodgates of despair,
    can result in the crafting of the notes of pending death.

The tongues of man speak to the heights of achievement,
    speak the vocabularies of The Saints,
    speak to The Glory of their God,
    speak the prayers of sinners,
    speak the greetings without shame,
    speak without hesitation to the calls upon their time.

The tongues of man sit on unuttered secrets,
    sit on conflicts coming to the boil,
    sit on hopes and expectations coming to fruition,
    sit on matters of the heart which should not be overlooked;
      which are not aired until the departure time arrives;
      which are not considered for an audience while it is today;
      which affect eternal lives when shyness dominates the
        kindred souls by freezing up the tongues."

Tongues of Demons (2)

The tongues of demons hold the curses and the spluttering,
        the vile and the disappointing,
        the crass and the profane,
        the lies and the tremors,
        the coarseness and the blasphemies:
                all to be so attributed to man.

The tongues of demons vilify and choke,
        recriminate and blame,
        regurgitate and shame,
        incriminate and lie.

The tongues of demons are heard in the sweatshops of The Earth,
        in the brothels serving man,
        in disowning the lead-up to the honeyed lie,
        in crafting believability into a course of action,
        in promising innocence to be the guardian of defence.

The tongues of demons are the marriage-breakers of The Earth,
        are the possessors and promoters of dissatisfaction,
        are the instructors of the inebriated,
        are the encouragers of the addicted,
        are the leaders into violence before taking a back seat.

The tongues of demons frequent the dilapidated and the dark,
        the gruesome and the grievous,
        the dank and the sweating,
        the secreted in the underground where dwell the
        compositors of the child and nude images:
                not meant for the light of day.

The tongues of demons speak in restricted tongues—
    tongues limited to the faction of society which find them carelessly attractive,
            which find them descriptive of their
                    way of life,
            which find the menial and the frivolous
            sufficient for their uses,
            which find the smug and the monied
                content with all the
                demons offer and support.

Revelation 6:1-8 plus Others

Revelation 6:1-2 Now I saw when the Lamb opened one of the seals; and I heard one of the four living creatures saying with a voice like thunder, "Come and see." ²And I looked, and behold, a white horse. He who sat on it had a bow; and a crown was given to him, and he went out conquering and to conquer.

Revelation 6:3-4 ³When He opened the second seal, I heard the second living creature saying, "Come and see." ⁴Another horse, fiery red, went out. And it was granted to the one who sat on it to take peace from the earth, and that people should kill one another; and there was given to him a great sword.

Revelation 6:5-6 ⁵When He opened the third seal, I heard the third living creature say, "Come and see." So I looked, and behold, a black horse, and he who sat on it had a pair of scales in his hand. ⁶And I heard a voice in the midst of the four living creatures saying, "A quart of wheat for a denarius, and three quarts of barley for a denarius; and do not harm the oil and the wine."

Revelation 6:7-8 ⁷When He opened the fourth seal, I heard the voice of the fourth living creature saying, "Come and see." ⁸So I looked, and behold, a pale horse. And the name of him who sat on it was Death, and Hades followed with him. And power was given to them over a fourth of the earth, to kill with sword, with hunger, with death, and by the beasts of the earth.

Revelation 7:11 All the angels stood around the throne and the elders and the four living creatures, and fell on their faces before the throne and worshiped GOD,

Revelation 15:7 Then one of the four living creatures gave to the seven angels seven golden bowls full of the wrath of God who lives forever and ever.

Revelation 19:4 And the twenty-four elders and the four living creatures fell down and worshiped God who sat on the throne, saying, "Amen! Alleluia!"

Scribal Note: *Refer to* Bk 2 'GOD Speaks to Man on The Internet': Revelation Ch 6:1-8 and Ch 10:1-11 Divine Commentary.
  Also: Fiery Red Horse,
  Refer Bk 2 'GOD Speaks to Man on The Internet': Revelation 6:4 Divine Commentary.

My Content Study Aid

_____
_____
_____
_____
_____

Four— Horses, Riders, Living Creatures

'My Lord, What is the precise connection between the four horses, the four riders, and the four living creatures?'

Divine commentary—
"All three divisions and all twelve perceptions, Anthony, My son, are one and the same.

They are all semblances of My Spirit: The Holy Spirit, The Enactor of My will, The Assessor of new life.

They each have ownership of periods of time, each with differing activities, each with differing purposes, but all cognizant of fulfilling the wrath, the vengeance, of God arising from the seven bowls of the seven angels which are also indicative of the perfection of Heaven and as semblances of the Holy Spirit. Do you understand, Anthony?"

'Yes, I think so, Lord. These related scriptural texts as found in The Book of Revelation and in your Divine Commentaries and your Parts of The End-time Psalms of God, or as The End-time Homilies of God, are all indicative of The Troubling of Man— the End-time Wrath of God— or, as man commonly refers to it— the Tribulation.'

Divine commentary—
"Yes, Anthony, you are correct in your understanding— of both the context and the content."

'Thank you, Lord.'

9.09 – 10.02 pm Saturday 24th December 2016

semblance|ˈsɛmbləns| noun *[mass noun]*
the outward appearance or apparent form of something, especially when the reality is different: *she tried to force her thoughts back into* **some semblance of** *order.*
• *archaic* resemblance; similarity: *it bears some* **semblance to** *the thing I have in mind.*
ORIGIN: Middle English: from Old French, from *sembler* **'seem'**, from Latin *similare, simulare* **'simulate'**.

Scribal Note: Fiery Red Horse,
Refer Bk 2 'GOD Speaks to Man on The Internet': Revelation 6:4 - Divine Commentary.

My Content Study Aid

_____

_____

_____

_____

The End-time Summary of God

"I,
   The Lord Jesus,
     survey The Multitudes this day,
     survey My people this day,
     survey the need for the End-time Psalms of God* to assist with the readiness of man,
          in the days of preparation,
             in the call to be ready to join The Bride of Christ,
             in the end-time where Faith and Grace prevail until the new dawn arises.

I,
   The Lord Jesus,
     present this book from within My dictation—
       where it has been sleeping—
       awaiting to come forth into the networks of man,
            into the social media in its fullness,
            into the trumpet call of God,
            into the world at loggerheads,
            into the world in turmoil,
            into the world of nation calls,
            into the world where unity has been split by the axe
                          of discord—
        surfacing from the voices of self-interest:
              those chasing self-aggrandizement—
     at the expense of those not permitted to feed at the tables of the gross
                          and selfish—
       who rule and reign without consideration for their fellow man.

I,
   The Lord Jesus,
     suffer all the children of the world to come unto Me—
       all those still young at heart,
       all those who care for and love their children too,
       all those who seek the beauty and the peace within a sanctuary,
       all those who would walk hand-in-hand with their God where joy and
                              love survive,
       all those who have not joined the barbarity of man.

I,
   The Lord Jesus,
     would step across the thresholds where an invitation is declared,
            where an invitation still exists within a heart,
            where an invitation comes to the fore when
                    musing on the reality of God.

I,
    The Lord Jesus,
        know when love is surfacing;
        know when love is proclaiming;
        know when love is present;
        know when love surmounts;
        know when love shares gratitude;
        know when love deepens,
                deepens,
                      deepens—
                              into the agapé love of God.

I,
    The Lord Jesus,
        am reaching out to man with the end-time urgency,
                with the offered hand of The Loving God,
                with the understanding and the knowledge
                      of the shortness of the breath of man,
                      of the dwindling sand now present within the hourglass
                                        of man,
                      of the proximity of man's farewell to Faith and Grace,
                      of the onset of the troubling of man—
                              who still carries sin—
                              who is not seated at The Table of The Lord—
                              who is not seated at the setting of The Bread
                                            and Wine.

I,
    The Lord Jesus,
        call for sacrifice of self,
        call for attention to a destiny,
        call for the forbearance of default,
        call for the commitment of man to his Loving God,
        call for man to make use of the mantles of Faith and Grace—
                and so achieve The Salvation of his soul;
                          The Redemption of his spirit;
                          The Justifying of his flesh:
                                as Righteousness is welcomed,
                                as My Spirit greets,
                                as the body of man becomes
                                      The Temple of The Living God."

Gratefully received from The Lord for use in this— both His first and ninth book.
    **or as 'The End-time Homilies of God'*
                        11.48 am – 12.38 pm Monday 19th December 2016

Journaling & Notes (1)

Journaling & Notes (2)

About The Scribe

Updated 16 March 2020

Anthony is 79, having been married to his wife, Adrienne, for 56 years. They have five married children: Carolyn, Alan, Marie, Emma and Sarah and fourteen grandchildren: Matthew & Ella; Phillipa & Jonathan; Jeremy, Ngaire & Trevor; Jake, Finn, Crystal & Caleb; Bjorn, Greta & Minka.

Anthony was raised on a dairy farm in Springston, Canterbury, NZ in the 1940s. He graduated from Canterbury University, Christchurch, NZ with a B.Sc. in chemistry and mathematics in 1962. He was initially employed as an industrial chemist in flour milling and linear programming applications.

These used the first IBM 360 at the university for determining least cost stock food formulations and production parameters. Later he was involved in similar applications on the refining side of the oil industry in Britain, Australia and New Zealand. This was followed by sales and managerial experience in the chemical industry.

The family moved to a Bay of Plenty, NZ, town in 1976 when Anthony took up funeral directing, as a principal, expanding an initial sibling partnership until the close of the century. Anthony acquired practical experience in accounting, business management, and computer usage (early Apples— including The Lisa).

Upon retiring from active funeral directing in 2000 and selling his interests, he then commenced the promotion and the writing of funeral management software for the NZ funeral environment. Rewarded with national success in NZ, with his son also expanding recently into Australia, he has now retired, in 2007, from the active management of that interest, as he quits it entirely in 2020. He lives near some of his family in Hamilton NZ.

Anthony was brought up in The Methodism of his father until his mid-teens, his mother's side was Open Brethren. He is Christian in belief within an Apostolic Pentecostal Charismatic framework of choice (since the 1990s) having been earlier in The Mormon church for several years. Thereafter he was in The Baptist denomination followed by finding a home within The Apostolic church movement.

He and his wife, who has visited a number of Asian countries, have been to India in 2011, 12, 13, 16 and 18 on The Lord's tasks and have witnessed and participated in many miracles which befall His People and The Multitudes.

His forbears William Henry Eddy and Margaret Jane Eddy, née Oats, emigrated to New Zealand from Gulval, Cornwall, England in 1878 on a sailing ship, with a very slow passage time of 79 days, and with their three month old infant child, Margaret Anne, dying 21 October 1878 from Congestion of the brain on board The Marlborough while en route to NZ. The Marlborough sailed London 19 September 1878, via Plymouth 26 September 1878, and arrived Lyttelton 14 December 1878 with 336 assisted immigrants. His grandfather, Alfred Charles Eddy, then but three years old, together with an older brother aged four, obviously survived the trials of the sea voyage to become a part of a family with a further eleven New Zealand born siblings all living to maturity.

Epilogue - 'Our GOD Lives'

9 Books of either The End-time Psalms of God*
or as The End-time Homilies of God

	Pages	Total Words
1. GOD Speaks of Return and Bannered	418	90,756
2. GOD Speaks to Man on The Internet	498	126,496
3. GOD Speaks as His Spirit Empowers	272	68,205
4. GOD Speaks to Man in The End-time	248	61,799
5. GOD Speaks in Letters of Eternity	236	57,257
6. GOD Speaks to His Bridal Presence	326	78,183
7. GOD Speaks to His Edifice	512	126,890
8. GOD Speaks of Loving His Creation	280	70,658
9. GOD Speaks Now of a Seal Revealed	124	24,528

Scribal Note: *These may probably be better known by man in his naming as 'The End-time Homilies of God - in being 'Religious discourses which are intended primarily for spiritual education rather than doctrinal instructions'.*

My Content Study Aid

4 Companion End-time Flowers of God

	Pages	Total Words
10. GOD End-time Updates Ancient Alien History	310	83,908
11. GOD End-time Updates His Call to The Multitudes	166	46,152
12. GOD End-time Updates The Bride of My Son	180	47,267
13. GOD End-time Updates The Guardianship of Friends	280	82,610

Synopses of The Flowers of God

Book Ten 'God End-time Updates Ancient Alien History' delves into the distant past of Flying Saucers with Alien strangers cross- and interbreeding to generate Neanderthals, and where the discovered new element of Moscovium disintegrates over time into an antigravity fuel, which enables flying saucers to fly the way they do, and where ancient knowledge tells of the extermination of the dinosaurs because of being predators. The current situation, with crop circles and Flying Saucers with real live Aliens, brings history up to date.

Book Eleven 'God End-time Updates His Call to The Multitudes' here The Lord Jesus speaks throughout The Earth— to all who would prepare for an ongoing life with Him. He is reaching out to have The Multitudes come to an understanding and awaits a response in answer to the question of the thoughtful: Why is The Freewill of man of such importance to God? Why is The Freewill of man such a determinant of the ultimate destiny of man? Why is The Freewill of man either respected or honoured by God? Why is The Freewill of man 'Honoured' by his movements within the new covenant?

Book Twelve 'God End-time Updates The Bride of My Son' as dictated by The Father. The Father loves and enfolds as He chooses to bring before The people of The Lord all those who are close to His Heart especially as the wisdom of the centuries has been nurtured in the heavens, is often obvious when spoken, raises eyebrows at the thoughts revealed, silences while matters are considered as to the best way forward. The wisdom of the centuries is a gift from God, is an enlightening of speech, is the victory of expression. The wisdom of the centuries is an expansion of vocabulary.

Book Thirteen 'God End-time Updates The Guardianship of Friends' with eighty six divinely selected scrolls dictated by Jesus: where The Curtain Call of God stimulates: in growth, in Faith, in righteousness, in expression, in quests, in being friendly and inviting. It affirms the value: of being under The Faith Field of Mortality, the confirmation of The Righteous Field of Morality, the requested availability of The Cleansing Field of Grace, the necessity of Seeking The Field of Preparation, The gifts of My Spirit as on The Day of Pentecost, the benefit of attaining fluency in The Heavenly Gift of Tongues, access to the given opportunity to select: the destiny of choice as the goal of life, to be so set in Faith for Freewill Activities— with Righteousness prevailing as the destiny is assured. It closes out the time of Grace, opens up the time of Mercy at The Bema Seat.

www.ingramcontent.com/pod-product-compliance
Lightning Source LLC
Chambersburg PA
CBHW060046230426
43661CB00004B/671